Research Notes for *Women at Play: The Story of Women in Baseball* Volume I: Maud Nelson Margaret Nabel

Barbara Gregorich

Cover design by Robin Koontz
Cover photo from postcard of Western Bloomer Girls
purchased in Watervliet, Michigan, circa 1990.

Gregorich, Barbara
Research Notes for Women at Play: The Story of Women in Baseball
Volume I: Maud Nelson, Margaret Nabel
CreateSpace Books

for Fred Schuld,
baseball fan, researcher, and friend

Introduction

I have been a baseball fan as far back as I can remember. The first book I wrote was a novel about a woman playing in the major leagues: *She's on First* was published in 1986. Two years later I started researching the history of women who played hardball and in March of 1993, *Women at Play: The Story of Women in Baseball* was published.

In the course of the fact finding and collecting, my notes multiplied to approximately 8,000 sheets of paper — including copies of old newspaper articles, transcribed notes from materials that could not be photocopied, interview notes, reproductions of photos, and so on.

Knowing that I couldn't write a book by referring to so many different notes, and knowing also that I couldn't keep that much information in my mind at all times, I adopted the plan of typing-up what I considered the salient information. I created scores of files on my computer, from "19th Century Baseball" to "Maud Nelson" to "Little League" to the "Sun Sox." From these condensed notes, with occasional forays into the 8,000 sheets of paper, I wrote *Women at Play*.

This method worked well for the project at hand. However, the notes weren't organized in chronological order. That task was too time-consuming for me back in 1992, when I was given exactly 92 days to write *Women at Play*. As a result, the better part of my labor in producing *Research Notes for Women at Play: The Story of Women in Baseball* consisted of creating historical order, so that the reader will have an easier time than I did following the course of events.

After *Women at Play* was published, I heard from relatives and friends of the women I had written about: nieces, nephews, great-nieces, great-nephews. Often these people sent me articles that I had not seen: I entered them into my data base if I considered them important or informative. Thus some of the articles here were added after 1993: wherever possible, I have indicated such.

My intention is to publish part of my baseball research notes in three volumes, the first of which is this one: *Research Notes for Women at Play: The Story of Women in Baseball: Volume I, Maud Nelson, Margaret Nabel,*

US copyright laws state that any newspaper article published prior to 1923 is in the public domain. Thus I have reproduced many original articles as they appear in my notes, from roughly 1875 through 1922. Wherever and whenever I knew the source, I have attributed it. Where I did not know the source, I have indicated "Source Unknown."

For articles printed in or after 1923, I've summarized the contents and quoted occasional lines.

In most cases I've tried to follow the headline style used by the newspaper quoted from. This makes for lack of uniformity in style, but helps give a more authentic feel to each article.

The section titled "Midwest Bloomers: Mostly Maud" contains articles that seem to be about Bloomer teams in general. But most of these pieces are clearly about Maud Nelson: they mention her by name. As to those that don't mention Maud . . . I leave it to future researchers to determine who was on that particular Bloomer team.

In quoting large blocks of text, I've followed the *Chicago Manual of Style 16th Edition* recommendation — I've indented the large blocks both left and right. In addition, I've justified the type of these large quoted sections. The indented text and justified type will make these direct quotations stand out.

Because I'm one of those people who jots notes in the margins of books (and because I believe that much written information is best absorbed when surrounded by ample "white space"), I've designed this volume with wide margins.

Finally, because the most exciting research I've ever done involves my discovering who Maud Nelson was, I have included "My Darling Clementine," an article about that extensive four-year search, at the end of this volume.

It is my hope that baseball researchers, baseball fans, and especially people interested in the history of women in baseball will find these notes valuable for their own research or simply their own knowledge.

It is also my hope that this volume may be of interest to libraries and to high school teachers or college instructors who teach writing the research paper. As a former teacher, I think such a volume would be a valuable resource.

Table of Contents

Before Maud

Baseball as played in the 1870s was, though thoroughly recognizable as baseball, different in many ways from today's game. Pitchers threw underhand, fifty feet from the plate. Catchers, standing behind the plate, caught the pitch on the bounce. Batters were out if the fielders caught the ball on the first bounce. Batters did not hold the bat at the end, nor did they take full swings: instead, they punched at the ball with the bat. Fielders didn't wear gloves. Home runs were rare. Scores were often higher than in today's games.

Young women organized baseball clubs at Vassar in 1866, playing in areas secluded from the public. In 1875, for the first time, women were paid to play baseball in public. This occurred in Springfield, Illinois. Soon thereafter promoters put together women's baseball teams and toured the East and South. Sometimes these teams included "ringers" — men dressed in women's clothing. Until the 1890s, however, most of these teams weren't very good.

1875

Daily State Journal, Springfield, Illinois, September 13, 1875
THE FEMALE BALL TOSSERS

This article reports on the game between the Blondes and the Brunettes, witnessed by a large crowd, with the playing field fenced off by a 9-foot high canvas fence.

The arrangement of the bases and field is a little over half that of the ordinary field, the bases being only fifty feet apart. The main features of the game were the catching of Sheila Brown of the 'Blondes,' the pitching of Jennie Wyman, on the same side, and the base running by Ledia Lambert. For the Brunettes Mollie Brodes pitched fairly, took in a fly, and Mollie Young on good batting secured three home runs. . . . Only six innings were played, and they occupied the full time. . . . The players conducted themselves like regular ballplayers — as much so as females can. The 'Blondes' . . . won the game by a score of 42 to 38.

New York Clipper, September 25, 1875
BLONDE vs. BRUNETTE
A Baseball Sensation

The first game of baseball ever played in public for gate money between feminine ball-tossers took place in Springfield, Ill., Sept. 11. The party who composed this "latest sensation" in the baseball arena include a selected troupe of girls of reputable character who have shown some degree of aptitude in ball-playing, and the arrangements are such as to include special bats and balls for the game they play, and a special field to play on, inasmuch as the ball is lighter, the bat smaller, and the field is reduced in size, the bases being located on a diamond-shaped field, the sides of which are but fifty instead of ninety feet from base to base. The troupe contains some pretty fair players, but as a general thing the attraction is the novelty of seeing eighteen girls prettily attired in gymnastic dress playing in a game of baseball. In the game at Springfield the Blondes won, as the appended score shows; but at Decatur the Brunettes won by 41 to 21, only six innings being played.

BLONDE	R	1B	E	BRUNETTE	R	1B	E
Eva Sheppard, 2d b	6	2	4	Anne Wilson, c	7	2	5
Emma Staeckling, rf	5	1	2	Josie Spencer, rf	7	1	1
Jane Wyman, p	6	1	5	Mary Young, ss	5	3	3
Mary Foster, lf	4	2	3	Louisa Chalmer, cf	3	0	0
Estella Brown, c	4	1	8	Maud Levi, 3d b	6	1	3
Eliza Sheppard, 3d b	4	0	4	Charlotte Clark, 2d b	4	0	4
Catherine Tinsly, 1 b	5	1	3	Ella Bergan, 1 b	2	0	2
Nettie Glidden, cf	3	0	2	Mary Braden, p	4	0	2
Lydia Lambeth, ss	5	3	4	Amy Bell, absent	0	0	0
TOTALS	42	11	35	TOTALS	33	7	20

Blonde .... 6 10 7 4 6 2 — 42
Brunette ...... 4 6 9 8 5 6 — 38

First-base by errors — Blonde, 13, Brunette, 9. Runs earned — Blonde, 3; Brunette, 1. Umpire, Mr. Stevenson. Time, 2h, 45m.

The runs in the box score, 42 to 33, do not correspond to the score reported in the article itself.

1883

New York Times, August 19, 1883

GIRLS AT BASE-BALL
A Ridiculous Exhibition
At a Philadelphia Park

PHILADELPHIA, Aug. 8 — At Pastime Park to-day 16 young girls, aided by two lads, played base-ball. There were about 500 spectators present, including a few ladies. The players were modestly dressed, and their skirts reached to their knees. One side wore dresses of white, with blue rimmings and stockings of a light red color, while the other had blue stockings. All wore jaunty little white cloth hats and base-ball shoes of the regulation style, except one girl, who luxuriated in 15-button gaiters that reached a span above her ankles and must have taken half an hour each to fasten. All had untanned belts around their little waists. Miss Williams, who acted as Captain of the reds, had a full suit of that color; and Miss Evans, who held similar command on the other side, showed a lovely outfit of cerulean blue and a little hat that had a flaunting blue ribbon. When play was called the reds went to the bat, each girl clamoring about the scorer's table to know when it would be her turn to "go in." It was evident from the start that the diamond of the regulation size was entirely too large for the girls either for running or throwing. A ball thrown from pitcher to second base almost invariably fell short, and was stopped on the roll. The throw from first to third base was an utter impossibility.

The throwing was a novelty at Pastime, and excited the players who watched the game to uncontrollable laughter. All the girls handled the ball in the same way. The right arm was doubled and the hand brought near to the face, then a sudden jerk threw it 80 feet or so. In catching all the girls held their hands out in front of them with the palms up; and, if the ball was well directed, and came at a nice curve, they caught it well enough, but if it came straight and fast their courage failed, and they got out of its way without delay. There were nine innings played, the reds making 34 runs and the blues 26. The young ladies have been only 10 days in practice. They are to play a game on Sept. 1 on a half-sized diamond, which will better suit their style of batting and throwing.

New York Times, September 23, 1883

A BASE-BALL BURLESQUE
BLONDES AND BRUNETTES TOYING WITH THE BAT
A Game in Which the Girl Players
Got Hopelessly Mixed and Furnished
Unlimited Fun to the Spectators

A crowd of about 1,500 people assembled on the Manhattan Athletic Club's grounds . . . yesterday afternoon, and laughed themselves hungry and thirsty watching a game of base-ball between two teams of girls. There were eight girls on a side, but there was more genuine circus in those 16 girls than is popularly supposed to reside in a Mormon colony. At 3:30 the two nines — or rather eights — entered the arena. One side was composed of brunettes, whose costumes were of an irritating red; the other was of blondes who wore sympathetic blue. The blondes won the toss and went to the bat with a air of determination…. The costumes were bathing dresses of the ancient and honorable order. The loose body had a long, flowing skirt, which reached below the knee. Stockings of the regulation style, base-ball shoes, and white hats completed the outfit. The dresses were neatly, but not gaudily, trimmed with white braid. The hair was either coiled tightly at the back of the head or worn in long plaits, tied up in ribbon of a color that pleased the wearer's fancy. Miss Williams, the blue pitcher, rejoiced in a natty blue and white cap, which gave her a business-like appearance.

These young ladies, as the management of the affair announced, were selected with tender solicitude from 200 applications, variety actresses and ballet girls being positively barred. Only three of the lot had ever been on the stage, and they were in the strictly legitimate business. . . . Most of the others were graduates of Sunday schools and normal colleges, who had seen the vanity of Greek and Latin and yearned to emulate the examples of the great and good students of Yale, Harvard, and Princeton by traveling wholly on their muscle. They were of assorted sizes and shapes.... They played base-ball in a very sad and sorrowful sort of way, as if the vagaries of the ball had been too great for their struggling intellects. They had started out in life with a noble ambition to "hang on" to anything that came from the bat, no matter how hot, and they had seen their dreams diminish as their bruises increased. Base-ball was not what it was painted, and they were evidently sighing for the end of the season. Four of the girls have become expert — for girls. These were Misses Evans, P. Darlington, Moore, and Williams, comprising the batteries. The others, however, had original ideas. They realized the fact that when they got hold of the ball they ought to throw it, and they threw. They didn't stop to wonder where the ball was going, for they were sure that it would not go too far. Each one just raised her hand to the level of her ear and then sent it forward with a push from the elbow. The ball didn't seem to mind it much. At the bat most of them preferred to strike at the ball after it passed them. Then it generally passed the catcher. First base was not made oftener than 15 times on three strikes. It was made just about as often on called balls. . . .

When the blues went to the bat Miss P. Darlington, pitcher for the reds, who stood about 20 feet in front of the striker, proceeded to tie up her back hair a little tighter. Then she put another hair-pin in her hat, seized the ball recklessly, drew back her right arm, and let fly viciously. Miss Moore responded gracefully by whacking a lively grounder to first base. The first basewoman made a wild grab, but did not touch the ball, whereupon the runner got around to third, while the other side pegged the ball all over the field. Finally Miss Williams went to the bat and hit a daisy cutter to short stop, who promptly threw it as far as she could into right field. [Immense applause.] Miss Moore ran home. The next striker, Miss Myers, made a one-base hit, which brought herself and Miss Williams home, owing to the futile attempts of the entire opposing nine to pick the ball up from the ground. The next three strikers were put out, and the brunettes went in. Miss Evans, who rejoiced in bright brown hair, was the genuine ball-player of the party. She warmed one to right field and made her second. Then Miss P. Darlington went in and hit a fly. . . .

. . . . The determined manner in which the brunettes staid in seemed to sadden the blondes; but, after a series of surprises, they were put out. Score of the first inning— Blondes, 3; Brunettes, 16.

It was a discouraging lead, but the blondes did not weaken. They went in and by determined efforts succeeded in scoring 2. They would have made a great many more, but Miss Evans, the brunette catcher, was a mean thing and would not indulge in passed balls like the other catcher, Miss Moore, who was a real nice girl. . . . Toward the end of the game the girls began to show symptoms of sadness and weariness, and doggedly refused to run from one base to another, until it became morally certain that the other side was hopelessly tangled up with the ball. Often, when the fielders could not stop the ball in any other way they sat down on it. This was at once effective and picturesque, and never missed gaining a great howl of applause. Once Miss Evans threw to second and put out Miss Brown. Then the crowd informed her that she was a "dumpling" and a "corker." . . . When five innings had been played, and the back hair and brains of the girls appeared to be in a hopelessly demoralized condition, with a tendency on the part of their hose to follow suit, the game was called. The girls heaved long sighs of relief, started for the dressing-rooms, and, "like an unsubstantial pageant faded, left not a pin behind." The score was 54 to 22 in five innings in favor of the brunettes. They play again tomorrow.

New York Tribune, September 23, 1883

    This article reports that the brunettes were dressed in red and the blondes in blue. "They wore trowsers gathered in at the knee and skirts coming just below the trowsers. . . . The game — but no one went to see the game — stood 51 to 22 at the end of the fifth inning. Then darkness put an end to the festivities."

1885

New Orleans Picayune, January 5, 1885
The League Clubs Keep Out of the Rain
But the Females Play

Women played baseball at the Sportsmen's Park with the T. S. Webers as opponents. The manager of the women's team was a man named Freeman. "Miss Lawrence and Miss Emerson were the battery."

New Orleans Picayune, January 12, 1885

Manager Freeman had a women's team in New Orleans and claimed they deserted him, "but that he will have another nine in the field, with a trip to Havana in prospect."

"However it be the New Orleans public do not seem to take kindly to female nines who cannot play ball, and the venture here has so far proved a failure."

Delta Atlas, Wauseon, OH, July 18, 1885

"Monday the Blondes and Brunettes played ball here against a nine of boys from 16 to 17 years of age. Nature wept. The score was 19 to 2 in favor of the boys."

My paper files contain many more short reports like the above, most of them from New Orleans, but the items are all so similar that I typed only a few into my computer files.

Midwest Bloomers: Mostly Maud

Maud Nelson, whose real name wasn't Maud and wasn't Nelson (see the article at the end of this book for more information), was the single most important influence on Bloomer Girl baseball during its existence. Bloomer Girl teams, named after the original baggy Amelia-Bloomer-type bloomers they wore, soon switched to regular baseball uniforms, which liberated them to hit, run, slide, and field more effectively. Most Bloomer teams consisted of six or seven women and two or three men.

On the front cover of this book, Maud Nelson is seated second from left.

1897

The Oregonian, Portland, OR, October 3, 1897
BLOOMERS PLAY BALL TODAY

The Boston Bloomers, ladies' champion baseball club of the world, will cross bats with the All-Portlands this afternoon at Portland field. These clever ladies put up an interesting and scientific game, full of fun and funny features. Judging from the many flattering notices they have received, the All-Portland nine will have to "play ball" to win. It is worth the price of admission alone to see Miss Nelson, the phenomenal pitcher. She has speed and curves. Game called at 3 o'clock.

The Oregonian, Portland, OR, October 4, 1897
BLOOMERS WERE BEATEN
"The Boston Bloomer baseball players were defeated by a local team on Portland field yesterday by a score of 12 to 8, but it took good playing to do it."

The article goes on to describe several plays and states that the Boston Bloomers consisted of eight women and one man, the catcher, "who hails from Washington, D.C., where, until lately, he has been putting up professional ball."

[The name of the catcher isn't given.]

Capital Journal, Salem, OR, October 5, 1897
THE BUFF BLOOMERS
The Boston Bloomer lady baseballists defeated the Scio Jefferson combination team by 10 to 9. The game was well contested. The Bostons have an excellent pitcher, are strong infield, and hard batters. Dr. Geo. Wright of McMinnville umpired.

They next play the Chemawa team at 11 a.m. Wednesday. About 1000 saw the game today and were highly pleased.

1899

Cincinnati Enquirer, July 9, 1899

The Bloomers lost to a local team in Elkton, Kentucky, by a score of 20 to 4.

Cincinnati Enquirer, July 11, 1899

The article calls the team the Bloomer Girls of Chicago. The Bloomers wcrc defeated by the Russellville, Kentucky, male team by a score of 13 to 3.

Cincinnati Enquirer, July 18, 1899

THE BLOOMER GIRLS AGAIN

Hopkinsville, KY, July 17 — A game of baseball played here this afternoon between the Bloomer Girls nine of Chicago and the Hopkinsville Club, resulted in victory for the home nine by score of 12 to 3.

1900

Cincinnati Enquirer, June 14, 1900

Knoxville, Tenn. June 13 — Five students of the University of Tennessee were to-day given notice of expulsion. Their offense was alleged connection with the management or playing of a game of baseball with the Chicago Bloomer Girls team in this city yesterday. Notice had previously been given that participation in this game would be followed by serious consequences. The students may appeal to the Trustees, who meet next Monday. Two were candidates for graduation next week.

Cincinnati Enquirer, June 27, 1900

The Bloomer Girls from Chicago were defeated by the Lancaster, Kentucky, baseball team, 15-14.

Cincinnati Enquirer, July 2, 1900

THE BLOOMERS OUTCLASSED

Special Dispatch to The Enquirer

Louisville, KY July 1 — Feminine science and pluck battled masculine brawn and muscle in a game of baseball yesterday afternoon, and to the credit of the former it must be said that, while it lost, it was not disgraced.

The contestants were the Bloomer Girls' baseball team and the Reccius local nine. While the game was one-sided from the standpoint of the runs earned and scored, still there were many good plays made on both sides, and in many instances plays bordering on the sensational were made.

While the girls are of good mettle and work industriously, and while the decisions of the umpire were anything but satisfactory, they were outclassed, and this alone accounts for the defeat by the score of 8 to 0.

Cincinnati Enquirer, July 21, 1900

GIRLS LOST, AS USUAL

Special Dispatch to The Enquirer

Jackson, Ohio, July 20 — To-day the Jackson baseball team defeated the Bloomer Girls, a traveling female aggregation of alleged ball players, in a game of languid interest by a score of 13 to 2.

Cincinnati Enquirer, August 18, 1900

BLOOMER GIRLS TRIMMED

Special Dispatch to The Enquirer

Marysville, Ohio, August 17 — The Chicago Bloomer Girls, a ball team composed of seven young ladies and two gents, played a very interesting game this afternoon with the Richwood nine on the latter's grounds in the presence of 1,500 spectators. The game resulted in a score of 10 to 3 in favor of Richwood. The ladies put up a great game and had an excellent battery. But for two costly errors they would have won. The ladies' battery was Miss Maud Nelson and Linsey pitchers and David Louis catcher. Richwood battery, Riley and McAdams did excellent work.

Cincinnati Enquirer, August 23, 1900

GALS WIN B'GOSH

Special Dispatch to The Enquirer

Union City, Ind., August 22 — The bloomer girls defeated the Union City team here to-day in a well-played game. The feature was the pitching of the Misses Maude Nelson and Edith Lindsay, only three hits being made off them. The score:

Innings	1	2	3	4	5	6	7	
Bloomer Girls	0	0	0	1	2	0	x	— 3
Union City	0	0	1	0	0	0	0	— 1

Hits — Bloomer Girls, 4; Union City, 2. Errors — Bloomer Girls, 2; Union City, 2.

Maud Nelson's name was sometimes spelled Maude *and sometimes* Maud. *Her last name was sometimes spelled* Nielson.

Cincinnati Enquirer, August 23, 1900

HOORAY FOR THE GIRLS

Versailles, Ohio, August 23 — The Chicago Bloomer Girls defeated the Versailles team here to-day in a well-played and interesting game. The feature was the pitching of Miss Maud Nelson, who is an expert in twisting the pig skin. The score stood 4 to 23 in favor of the Bloomers. **Batteries — Nelson and Jones; Searles and Coughlin.**

Cincinnati Enquirer, August 25, 1900

BLOOMER GIRLS LOST

Covington, Ohio, August 24 — The Bloomer Girls and Covington Pets played an interesting and hotly contested game here today. The score: Bloomers, 2; Covington, 5. **Batteries: Brown, Russell and Nelson; Hudson and Riddle.** Attendance: 1,200. Miss Nelson's pitching was one of the main features of the game, while the Covington team upheld their enviable record of not being defeated this season, and expect to be in the game in earnest next Monday when they meet the Reds.

Cincinnati Enquirer, August 26, 1900

LOST GAME, BUT MADE MONEY

Celina, Ohio, August 25 — Over 500 people saw the Celinas defeat the Bloomer Girls at the fair grounds park this morning. The features of the game were Miss Nelson's pitching and the third base playing of Miss Lindsay. Following is the score:

Innings	1	2	3	4	5	6	7	8	9	
Celina	1	0	0	1	0	8	0	0	0	— 10
Bloomer Girls	0	0	0	2	0	0	1	0	2	— 5

Batteries — Celina, Webber and Hardin; Bloomer Girls, Nelson, Lindsay and Jones.

Cincinnati Enquirer, August 29, 1900

A report from from Upper Sandusky, Ohio, indicates that the Bloomer Girls were defeated at Sycamore 7-3.

Cincinnati Enquirer, September 3, 1900

SHUT THE BLOOMERS OUT

Delphos, Ohio, September 2 — "The Bloomer Girls' ball team was given its first shut-out this season by the locals in a swift game." Attendance was 3,000 people.. Score:

Innings	1	2	3	4	5	6	7	8	9		
Bloomer Girls	0	0	0	0	0	0	0	0	0	—	0
Delphos	0	0	1	3	3	6	1	0	x	—	14

Hits — Bloomer Girls, 5; Delphos, 11. Errors — Bloomer Girls, 9; Delphos, 1. Batteries — Misses Nelson and Lindsay; Martin and Jones; Davis and Jettinger. Struck Out— By Martin, 1; by Davis, 9. Umpire — Roth.

Cincinnati Enquirer, September 22, 1900

From Ottawa, Ohio, September 1— The Bloomer Girls were defeated by the local team in an exciting seven-inning game. The score was 4-3, favor of Ottawa. The Bloomer Girls had 3 hits, 3 runs, 5 errors. Ottawa had 3 hits, 4 runs.

1903

Cincinnati Enquirer, July 20, 1903

BLOOMER BALL TOSSERS
Were Pinched, and Raised a Rough
House in Texas Jail

Special Dispatch to The Enquirer

Dallas, Texas, July 19 — A club of female ballplayers, claiming to be from Brooklyn, N.Y., were jailed at Ft. Worth to-day for persisting in playing a game with a club of young men, after being notified by the police that the city park could not be held for ball-playing purposes. The bloomer aggregation became "sassy" and was run in. The only names given were Josie Coleman, Verda Hall and May Terry. The others were docketed as unknowns. In the corridors and cells the girls raised a "rough house." They sang up-to-date topical songs, roasted the jail officials and male prisoners, turned handsprings, stood on their heads, walked on their hands, did high kicking, wide splits and other startling performances. After a lapse of two hours' time a party of sporting men secured their release on time. A spicy time is looked for at the trials before the Police Justice to-morrow.

Boston Herald, August 23, 1903

WOMAN PLAYS GREAT BALL
Miss Neilson, Although Her Team Lost,
Struck Out Seven Men in Five
Innings and Hit Hard

Special Dispatch to the Sunday Herald.

Lewiston, Me., Aug. 22, 1903 — The Star Bloomers, an aggregation consisting of three men and six women, played a game of baseball this afternoon on Garcelon Athletic Field with the Athletics of this city. The Athletics won by a score of 9 to 8. The feature of the game was the pitching, batting and fielding of Miss Neilson. She made three base hits, and had four put outs and four assists and made no errors. In the five innings she pitched she struck out seven men. One thousand people witnessed the exhibition. Score:

Innings	1	2	3	4	5	6	7	8	9		r.	h.	e.
Athletics	0	1	1	1	0	0	5	0	1	—	9	12	4
Bloomer Girls	0	2	0	1	0	0	0	0	5	—	8	9	6

Batteries — Sutton and Joyce; Neilson, McKenzie and McDonald.

1904

I received the two Cleveland Leader *articles years after* Women at Play *was published.*

Cleveland Leader, June 17, 1904

DEFEAT FOR BLOOMER GIRLS

Sharon, Penn., June 16 — (Special.) — One of the largest crowds of the season saw the Independents win a farcical game from the Star Bloomer Girls by a score of 16 to 13 [*sic*] to-day. The home players gallantly allowed the six women and three men opponents to make runs and tried to make the contest interesting by putting nearly every man on the nine either on the rubber or behind the home plate. Score:

										R.	H.	E.
Sharon	2	0	1	3	1	0	3	6	0 —	16	22	0
Bloomer girls	2	0	1	0	2	0	2	1	4 —	12	13	6

Batteries — Nelson, McKenzie, and Florn: Rudelph, Cream, East, Clayson, and Gibson.

Cleveland Leader, June 23, 1904

BLOOMER GIRLS ARE DEFEATED

Geneva, Ohio, June 23 — (Special.) — Geneva defeated the Bloomer Girls here today in a well-played game. Their team was composed of five girls, the others being men. Geneva's new battery, Sargent and Allen, did good work. Score:

										R.	H.	E.
Geneva	0	0	0	0	1	0	0	3	0 —	4	9	5
Bloomer Girls	0	0	0	0	1	0	0	0	0 —	1	3	6

Batteries — Geneva, Sargent and Allen; Bloomer Girls, Nelson and Langhren.

1905

Maud Nelson was married to John B. Olson, Jr., and traveled with him and the Cherokee Indian Base Ball team, some years pitching, some years not.

Watervliet Record, Watervliet, MI, February 3, 1905

J.B. OLSON PURPOSES TO MAKE WATERVLIET HEADQUARTERS FOR HIS AMUSEMENT ENTERPRISES.

This article reports that John B. Olson purchased the Lottridge Farm near the village of Watervliet. and that he arrived from Chicago Heights, Illinois, with a Pullman car. It also states that Olson would make Watervliet his headquarters.

The coach is a combination sleeping and dining car and will be used the coming season for the accommodation of Mr. Olson's "Indian Baseball Team." The troupe will consist of eighteen people and will start from Watervliet in May after two weeks' training here. He will build an under-compartment to the coach this winter to hold the circus seats and other paraphernalia. He carries a complete canvas fence and portable grandstand for use in towns having no inclosed ball park. The team will travel through Michigan, New York and Canada and be gone all summer.

Watervliet Record, Watervliet, MI, March 3, 1905
This piece of news reports that John B. Olson rented his farm to Hugh Wigent.

Watervliet Record, Watervliet, MI, April 14 , 1905

Mr. L. C. Figg and wife arrived here from Chicago last week and will remain until the 'Cherokee Indian Base Ball Team,' of which Messrs. Olson and Figg are proprietors, starts on its tour about May 1st. They have thoroughly overhauled and refitted the interior of their Pullman car, 'Clementine" . . . . They will carry eleven Indian base ball players, besides four canvas men and the proprietors and their wives and all will eat and sleep on the car.

The canvas fence was 1200 feet long and 12 feet high "for use in towns that have no enclosed grounds." The portable grand stand would seat 1,000 people. The Pullman car would also carry a complete lighting plant for night games. The team would travel through Michigan, Canada and New York during the summer and would possibly play through the South and in Cuba next winter.

Watervliet Record, Watervliet, MI, May 5, 1905

Olson & Figg's Cherokee Indian team left Watervliet to play Grand Rapids, then Kalamazoo. "Five Indians from Detroit, Minnesota, are expected to join the team. . . . Francis Quigno of North Watervliet will go as a member of the team and John Herron will also go with the company."

Watervliet Record, Watervliet, MI, May 12, 1905
CHEROKEES MEET DEFEAT AT GRAND RAPIDS

The Cherokee Indian baseball team lost to the Grand Rapids Greulichs, 6-1. The article reports that two or three of the best Cherokee players had not yet arrived to join the team. "Numerous errors by the Redmen accounted for most of the runs made by the locals. . . ."

Watervliet Record, Watervliet, MI, May 26, 1905

"Mrs. J. B. Olson and son arrived here this week from Anderson, Ind. Mrs. Olson will rejoin the Cherokee Indian Base Ball Club in a week or ten days, but the boy will remain here. The club has seen some very poor baseball weather so far, but notwithstanding has done a fairly good business."

Eddie Olson, John's son from a previous marriage [to Lena Bowe], most likely stayed with his grandparents, John Sr. and Rachel Olson. Eddie was born in 1895 in Chicago, so he was ten at this time.

Watervliet Record, Watervliet, MI, July 7, 1905

Francis Quigno left the team at Buffalo and returned to Watervliet.

Sometimes the Watervliet Record *indicated that Buffalo was the New York city, and sometimes, as above, it did not indicate such. Perhaps sometimes it was, and sometimes it wasn't: that is, another Buffalo may have been meant. When the* Watervliet Record *indicated "New York," I indicate so in my notes.*

Watervliet Record, Watervliet, MI, August 11, 1905

John Olson arrived home for a brief stay. The Cherokees played at Howard City, MI, the previous day.

Cincinnati Enquirer, October 6, 1905

THE BLOOMER GIRLS
Easily Defeated the Cincinnati Stars
Yesterday — Score 12 To 7

Before a large crowd at the Cumminsville Ball Park, the Star Bloomer Girls defeated the Cincinnati Stars by the score of 12 to 7. The girls played as if their lives depended on winning the game and though they were up against one of the strongest amateur teams in the city they never showed the white feather, but kept working hard for victory.

On the other hand the gentleman ball team playing under the name of Cincinnati Stars, after making four runs in the first inning, got careless and the fair ones had the boys at their mercy. It was simply a case of follow-me, boys, as the Bloomer Girls forged ahead with four runs and added three more to their score before they left the field. Maud Ncilson pitched the first four innings and the boys made four runs off her slants and shoots. She stated she was not feeling well before the game, having been on the road for the past two weeks and for that reason was not in the best of condition. But at that, if it had not been for two unfortunate errors by the right fielder, the boys would have made but one run off her delivery. McKenzie finished the game and pitched gilt-edged ball. Only three hits were made off his delivery in the next five innings and one of them was a fluke. The work of Miss Day at first was a revelation to the large crowd in attendance. No matter where the ball was thrown she would get it. Some of her pick-ups of low-thrown balls were remarkable. She also led her side in batting. Miss Grace, in right field, made a hit with the bleachers with her fast work on bases and was picked out by the bleacherites as "The Peach" of the bunch.

At second Miss Dolly got everything that came her way and figured in two double plays. The other girls did their share in helping to down the Cincinnati Stars. . . .

The score:

BLOOMER GIRLS	AB	H	PO	A	E	CIN'TI STARS	AB	H	PO	A	E
Miss D., 1b	4	2	5	0	1	Fer'n, p-cf	4	1	8	6	0
Miss D'g, ss	4	2	2	1	1	Ryan, c	4	1	10	1	0
M's M., 3b-p	3	3	1	5	0	O'Br'n, 1b-p	4	1	3	3	0
Miss J'n., 1f	4	1	1	1	2	Reggy, 2-b	3	1	3	3	1
Miss T'k., c	5	2	10	0	0	Shulte, ss	3	1	0	2	0
M's N., p-3b	3	1	2	3	0	Chev'er, 3b	4	1	0	4	0
Miss D., 2b	4	0	3	1	1	Sch'ly, lf-c	4	1	8	6	0
Miss G., rf	3	1	0	0	0	Lloyd, cf-p	3	2	0	4	0
Miss M'e., cf	4	1	0	0	0	O'Con'or, rf	4	1	2	0	0
TOTALS =	34	12	27	11	5		32	10	27	20	2

Innings	1	2	3	4	5	6	7	8	9		
Bloomer Girls	0	0	0	3	0	3	4	2	0	—	12
Cincinnati Stars	4	0	0	0	1	0	1	1	0	—	7

Two-Base Hits— Teck, Schelbly, O'Brien. Three-Base Hit — Darling. Home/Run — McKensie. Struck Out — By McKensie, 8; by Lloyd, 3; by Ferguson, 5. Time — 1:40. Umpire — Mike Devanney.

Cincinnati Enquirer, October 7, 1905

TO TOUR THE WORLD

Bloomer Girls May Play Baseball Abroad

The second game of the series between the Bloomer Girls and the Cincinnati Stars was won by the Stars in easy fashion. The Stars had on their batting clothes and hit the ball hard and often. Reggy, Ryan, Schulte, Prout and Lloyd were there when hits meant runs. The boys also showed up much stronger in their fielding than they did the day previous at the Cumminsville Park. Schulte and O'Brien excelled in this respect. Ferguson as usual pitched his mately game and not a run was made off him in the five innings that he pitched. The Bloomer Girls fielded nicely at times, but were weak at the bat, except in one inning. Manager Schmelz certainly has a jewel in Miss Day at first base. She is without doubt the greatest lady ball player in the business and deserves all the nice things that have been said by the press throughout the country about her. Darling at short and McKenzie in the outfield could give some of the stars in the Central League cards and spades and beat them out. They also know how to hit the ball. Quite a large crowd saw the game. Both teams play the last of the series today at the Covington Ball Park, and will no doubt pack the stands. "This will be our last trip for two years," said Manager Schmelz of the Bloomer Girls, "in this part of the country, as we intend to make an extended trip through Cuba and Australia, and may go as far as England." The following is yesterday's score:

Innings	1	2	3	4	5	6	7	8	9		
Bloomer Girls	0	0	0	0	0	3	1	0	1	—	5
Cincinnati Stars	0	9	0	3	4	0	1	0	1	—	18

 Three-Base Hits — Reggy, Schulte, Schelbly and Prout. Two-Base Hits— Reggy, Schulte, Schelbly and Darling. Time— 1:35. Batteries — Cincinnati Stars, Ferguson, Chevelier and Ryan; Bloomer Girls, McKenzie, Neilson and Tueck. Umpire — Devaney.

Watervliet Record, Watervliet, MI, October 20, 1905
This item reports that John and Maud have returned to their farm.

1906

Watervliet Record, Watervliet, MI, January 26, 1906

J.B. Olson returned last Sunday from a two weeks' search for his private car that he had leased to a show company. He found the car at some point in Illinois, the parties to whom he had leased it having repainted it, causing him considerable trouble in locating it.

Watervliet Record, Watervliet, MI, April 20, 1906

This article reports that John Olson was fitting the Pullman car for his annual tour with the Cherokee Indian Baseball Club. The team would be managed by Olson and McMillan this season and they expected to start from Chicago on May 1.

Watervliet Record, Watervliet, MI, May 4, 1906

"Manager Olson has arranged for a game with Hartford [Michigan] for Friday afternoon, May 11, at the Hartford ball grounds. Busses and automobiles will furnish transportation from Watervliet at a low rate for the round trip and admission to the game is only 25 cents." The article reports that this is the first time in years that Watervliet has had a contending team against Hartford. "Hartford has engaged a strong battery from abroad to play with their team this season and they will undoubtedly put up a warm game, but Manager Olson is confident the Indians will win."

Hartford Daily Spring, Hartford, MI, May 9, 1906

This item reports on the coming game between the newly organized Hartford team and the Cherokee Indians, managed by John B. Olson. "The Indians travel in their own private car and carry a complete outfit for playing both day and night games."

LOCALS LOST INITIAL GAME
Hartford Suffered Defeat at the Hands
of the Cherokee Indians Friday

Cherokee Indians 14
Hartford 6

The base ball season was given an auspicious opening in Hartford last Friday when the local bunch was handed a defeat by the Cherokee Indian team. Not that it might not have been more auspicious had Manager Greenfield's hopefuls placed a victory to their credit in the initial game, but this was hardly to be expected considering the speed of their opponents. They played good ball, and the form they displayed in the first game of the year is sufficient assurance that they will be handling the sphere in a really scientific manner before the season is far advanced.

Nearly 400 people witnessed the contest, Hartford, Watervliet and Coloma being well represented. Many of them passed in their quarters at the gate with the conviction that they were purchasing a 25 cent farce, but they were disappointed. While the victory was decisive it was far from a farce. Both teams played ball, and Hartford made a sufficient showing against the speedy Indian aggregation to satisfy the fans.

The Cherokees went to bat first and chalked up three scores in the opening inning. A part of the crowd murmured a faint "I told you so." But Hartford came to bat, pounded out four safe hits and tied the score. Another part of the crowd braced up.

In the second the Indians captured another tally, while Hartford went out in one, two, three order. In the third the program was reversed and Hartford took one.

Things went wrong in the fourth and the Indians claimed credit for four runs while Hartford took one. The balance of the game was more even, although the Indians failed to score in the sixth inning only, while Hartford couldn't succeed in crossing the plate again until the ninth — leaving the final score 14 to 6.

Doctor, the Indian pitcher, threw a good game and showed excellent control. But the locals had his measure and every man on the team, with the exception of two, placed safe hits to their credit. Quigno, who twirled for the locals, also pitched a good game in many respects, although his wildness permitted six men to saunter down to first. He placed nine strikeouts to his credit, however, while only seven were accorded his opponent.

The complete score of the opening game follows.

CHEROKEE INDIANS	AB	R	H	0	A		HARTFORD	AB	R	H	0	A
Cote, l	6	2	1	16	1		Straub, 2	5	0	2	6	1
Charles, s	6	3	2	0	3		Hill, 1	5	0	1	6	0
Bla'k, cf, m	6	3	2	1	0		Moore, m	5	1	0	2	0
Kirke, 3	6	1	2	0	4		Jackson, r	4	2	1	0	
J. Scrogge 2	6	1	2	1	3		Bennett, s	4	1	2	1	0
H. Scrog'e,1	6	1	2	1	0		Martin, 3b	4	0	2	1	0
Sprague, r	6	1	0	0	0		Johnson, l	4	0	1	2	1
Fish, c	5	0	1	8	1		Quigno, p	4	0	0	1	0
Doctor, p	5	1	2	0	5		Castor, c	4	2	2	8	2
TOTALS =	52	14	14	27	16		TOTALS =	39	6	11	27	10

Innings

Cherokee Indians	3	1	4	1	0	1	2	2	—	14
Hartford	3	0	1	1	0	0	0	3	—	6

Errors — Charles, 2, Kirke, 2, J. Scragge; Straub 2. Hill 2. Martin, Quigno, Castor. Sacrifice hits — Cote, Charles. Two base hits — Kirke, H. Scrogge, Bennett. Base on balls — Off Quigno 6. Struck out — By Doctor 7, by Quigno 9. Umpires Smith and Johnson.

In the above box score there are too many errors for me to add sic *to. Right fielder Jackson is not credited for one of his stats, most likely Assists. The total of 10 Hartford assists indicates that Jackson probably had six assists.*

The total innings listed are eight, not nine. No inning number is given, so I don't know which inning is missing. The score of the eight innings listed does not add up to 14 runs for the Cherokee Indians. I assume that the final score, 14-6, is correct.

The name of Scrogge is misspelled. The list of baseball errors appears to be mispunctuated and is certainly confusing. There may be other errors (typo, not baseball) that I have failed to mention.

Watervliet Record, Watervliet, MI, May 18, 1906

The Cherokee Indians lost to the Chicago Neutrals the previous Sunday in an 11-inning game, 3-2. The team will remain in Chicago all week and will play the Leland Giants.

Watervliet Record, Watervliet, MI, May 25, 1906

The Cherokee Indians lost to the Chicago Artesians, a semipro team, 6-0. "Harry Litman pitched one of the best games ever twirled by a semi-professional pitcher yesterday at his own park against the Cherokee Indians, holding the red men to one hit."

Watervliet Record, Watervliet, MI, July 20, 1906

John Olson wrote to friends saying the Cherokee Indians were meeting "with splendid success both professionally and financially."

Des Moines Register and Leader, July 30, 1906

According to the article, by this date the Cherokees had won 69 out of 74 games. The article says the players are all Indians from reservations. This article is accompanied by a photo showing the team, managers, and mascot. J.B. Olson is listed as manager, as is F. McMillan, and Eddie Olson is listed as the mascot.

Des Moines Register and Leader, August 5, 1906

INDIANS DEFEAT YEOMEN

The Cherokee Indian team won, 8-3, with batteries Emerson and Fish. This game was played on August 4, with an afternoon game scheduled for August 5. The Yeomen sought to strengthen their team by importing players from larger city.

The Yeomen won the second game, 1-0, in "the fastest amateur game ever seen in Des Moines." Time of game, :55 minutes. The Yeomen pitcher struck out 8, and Williams, the Cherokee pitcher, struck out 9. The Yeomen stole two bases, Indians 1. The Yeomen got 7 hits, Indians 4. Earned runs, Yeomen, 1.

Most of the players on the Cherokee Indian Base Ball team were Native Americans, though not necessarily Cherokees. In my summaries of these newspaper articles I sometimes use the term Indians *to refer to the entire team by name, and sometimes I use the term* Cherokees *to refer to the entire team by name. In all cases I'm referring to the baseball team itself, not to the nationality or tribe of the players.*

Watervliet Record, Watervliet, MI, August 12, 1906

This piece reports on a letter from Iowa from John, in which he enclosed a number of clippings showing how well the Cherokee Indian Base Ball Club was doing. The team played two games in Kingsley, Iowa, on July 4 and won both, with 4,000 people attending, the game being the chief attraction of the celebration. This was the fastest game ever played at Kingsley. The *Omaha Bee* of July 29 reported that the Cherokees won 1-0 and 6-4 against the Athletics. The Cherokee Indians team was highly praised for its playing.

Watervliet Record, Watervliet, MI, September 28, 1906

J.B. Olson, Jr. and family expect to arrive home about October 7. They will close the season with the Cherokee Indian Base Ball Team with a game at Chicago about Oct. 4. The Cherokee Indians have toured Illinois, Iowa and Nebraska and have had a most successful season.

Watervliet Record, Watervliet, MI, October 5, 1906

A news piece reports that the Olsons returned Tuesday [which would have been October 2].

1907

Watervliet Record, Watervliet, MI, January 11, 1907

John's railroad coach, which had been standing in the yards since the close of baseball season, "narrowly escaped destruction by fire last Saturday night. The blaze is supposed to have started from the spontaneous combustion of oily rags." The blaze was discovered and promptly extinguished. Damage amounted to about $25.

Watervliet Record, Watervliet, MI, February 8, 1907

Mrs. John B. Olson, Sr. , who had been visiting relatives at Stavanger, Norway, for the past three months, was expected home in a few weeks.

Watervliet Record, Watervliet, MI, March 22, 1907

"Olson and McMillan are busy making arrangements for their summer tour with the Cherokee Indian Base Ball team. . . . A new feature this year will be an Indian Band of ten pieces which they will carry with them." The players will arrive about April 20 for ten days practice and "J. B. Olson will arrange with some good local team for a game at Watervliet before they start on their tour."

Watervliet Record, Watervliet, MI, May 3, 1907

Indian Ball Team Will Organize at
Watervliet Again this Spring

Olson & McMillan are busy making arrangements for their summer tour with the Cherokee Indian Base Ball team and they will organize the team here again this spring. A new feature this year will be an Indian Band of ten pieces which they will carry with them. Mr. Olson expects his ball players and the members of his band to arrive here about April 20th for a ten-days' practice and he will arrange with some good local team for a game at Watervliet before they start on their tour.

Watervliet Record, Watervliet, MI, May 3, 1907

Cherokee Indians Play Ball with
Hartford To-Day

Olson & McMillan have 22 Indians here now comprising the ball team and members of the band. They have arranged with Manager Olds of Hartford for a game with the Hartford team on the Hartford grounds this afternoon. Hartford is planning to get even with the Indians for doing them up a year ago and besides five of their best home players, Bennett, Straub, Martin, Moore and Johnson, they have engaged Rawson of Decatur to pitch, Harkrider of Benton Harbor to catch, Eckhurst of Decatur and Jennings of Lawrence. Manager Olson believes he has the fastest team of Indian ball players that he ever started out with and the chances are that Hartford will suffer another defeat at the hands of the Cherokee Indians of Watervliet.

Mr. Olson intends to leave with his car Saturday for Chicago where they will play Sunday.

Hartford Daily Spring, Hartford, MI, May 8, 1907

The Cherokees won in a 7-inning game by the score of 5-0. Abrams was the Indian pitcher. Lineup: Cote, Jimerson, Jacobs, Grant, Lewis, Lay, Quigno. The game was called at end of seventh due to rain.

Watervliet Record, Watervliet, MI, May 10, 1907

Cherokee Indians Defeat Hartford
5 to 0. Lose Two Games in
Chicago Sunday

Olson & McMillan's Cherokee Indians played their first game of the season at Hartford last Friday, winning by a score of 5 to 0. It was a good game, neither side making a score after the first inning. On account of the rain, only seven innings were played. Hartford had a team of good players, but they were unable to get any safe hits off from Olson's left-handed pitcher.

The car "Clementine" with the band and ball team left here Saturday morning for Chicago where they played two games Sunday. They lost the game to the Phelix Colts by a score of 8 to 1 and to the Harlems by a score of 9 to 3.

The brass band of Indian players, uniformed in Indian costume, proves an added attraction to their games this season.

Watervliet Record, Watervliet, MI, July 12, 1907

Word comes from Pennsylvania that the Cherokees are playing good baseball.

Watervliet Record, Watervliet, MI, September 20, 1907

This article reports that a team called the All-Chicagos was organized by four men to tour the South that winter in a private car named Tioga.

Holland City News, Holland, MI, September 26, 1907

This article reports that the Cherokee Indian Base Ball Team was coming to Holland and "will bring with them their own tent and their own outfit, and will play two games of baseball with the Interurbans next Friday. One will be played in the afternoon and one in the evening in the great tent lighted by the electric lights which the company carries the equipment to operate."

Watervliet Record, Watervliet, MI, September 27, 1907

CHEROKEE INDIANS CLOSE SEASON
AT BANGOR SATURDAY AFTERNOON

This article reports that Olson & McMillan's Cherokees arrived home after a 6-month tour and will close the season with an afternoon and night game at Bangor. "Mr. McMillan, who does the advance work, arrived here the latter part of last week. A number of Watervliet people are planning to go to Bangor tomorrow and see the game."

John wrote to Postmaster Spreen and stated that they would like to see many of their friends at the afternoon game at Bangor on Saturday. "He writes that the boys have been playing good ball and that he is more than pleased with his trip this season; he writes further that he has seen all of the East that he cares to — 'Michigan for mine.'"

Holland City News, Holland, MI, October 3, 1907

Francis Quigiree, a member of the Cherokee Indian team, . . . dropped a pocketbook containing $73.80 in Japinga's saloon and William Verhey, a mason, picked it up and pocketed it. When the Indian missed the money he was told by an eye witness who had it and the matter was reported to Chief Kamferbeek — Verhey denied having the purse, but when told that arrest stared him in the face he returned it to police headquarters and admitted his guilt.

Watervliet Record, Watervliet, MI, October 4, 1907

BIG CHIEF HELD UP
Cherokee Indian Loses $73 in Holland Saloon,
but J. B. Olson Recovers the Dough

While the Cherokee Indian Ball Team was at Holland last Friday one of the Indians got mixed up with too much firewater and either lost or had stolen from him in a saloon, his pocketbook containing $73. J. B. Olson went to the saloonkeeper and says: "The Indian lost 73 bucks here, here's where the 'booze' was shot into him. I am coming back Monday and you had better have the money ready for me." It was an effective play. The saloonkeeper put the police next to the party who had the pocketbook and they recovered it. Monday Mr. Olson received a telephone [*sic*] that the money was there for him and he and the Indian went to Holland and got it.

Watervliet Record, Watervliet, MI, October 25, 1907

This article reports that John Olson picked 120 bushels of fine apples from his orchard.

Mr. Olson only recently returned from his base ball tour and had hardly got in touch with his farming operations so before he knew what they were worth he took 3400 pounds of fine apples to the cider mill and had them ground up. When he learned that the scrubbiest kind of apples were selling for one dollar a bushel he regarded his two barrels of cider with anything but pleasing contemplation.

Watervliet Record, Watervliet, MI, November 1, 1907

Wednesday morning J. B. Olson drank several swallows of turpentine, mistaking it for medicinal water. He was badly frightened at first thinking he had drank carbolic acid. When he realized that it was turpentine he thought he might have a chance for his life and rushed to the telephone and called a physician who prescribed hot water and salt and John said he drank a barrel of it. He suffered no serious results from the drink of turpentine.

Watervliet Record, Watervliet, MI, November 15, 1907

John Olson returned from deer hunting in the Upper Peninsula where he had gone with three others, because there were so many more hunters than deer "that it is dangerous to be out in the woods." Olson and Lottridge were shot at.

Watervliet Record, Watervliet, MI, November 15, 1907

Mrs. J. B. Olson and son Eddie, and nephew, Alphonse Brida, returned Saturday from a few days' visit in Chicago.

1908

Watervliet Record, Watervliet, MI, January 3, 1908
J. B. OLSON PURCHASES ROSSA VILLA
One of the Prettiest Hotel Properties
on Paw Paw Lake Becomes
Possession of Base Ball Man

This front-page item reports that the villa and the five acres of land that went with it were purchased by John B. Olson, Jr. The hotel was located at the west end of Paw Paw Lake near Will-o-Paw. A resort hotel, "the house contained 28 rooms finished in birdseye maple and handsomely furnished. The consideration is $3,500. Mr. Olson's mother will manage the hotel the coming season."

The article also reports that Olson will travel to Chicago in a few days to meet his partner, Mr. McMillan, and "make arrangements for the 1908 tour of the Cherokee Indian Ball Team."

Watervliet Record, Watervliet, MI, January 31, 1908
John and Maud spend the week in Chicago.

This article contains a picture of Rose Villa and reports that it accommodates 50 guests, rates $7 per week. Fruits and vegetables for the tables would be grown on the Olson farm, and milk would come from the farm, also.

Watervliet Record, Watervliet, MI, March 20, 1908
John went to Buffalo, New York, to "engage some fast Indian ball players" to play for his team this year.

Watervliet Record, Watervliet, MI, April 24, 1908
This piece reports that John Olson expects members of his team to arrive around the first of May and that they will practice in Watervliet for a couple of weeks.

Watervliet Record, Watervliet, MI, May 15, 1908

This article is accompanied by a picture of Maud Nelson in baseball uniform. It reports that the Cherokee Indian night game against Hartford would be played on a 60-foot diamond. The report states that this year the Cherokee Indian team,

assisted by Bob Rothermel, their trainer and advisor, and a player of the National League game, will play a game at Hartford, Mich., on Friday, May 15, at 3 P.M. and also a night game under a glare of 50,000 candle power light.

In connection with these two games, Maude Nelson, who enjoys the distinction of being the undisputed Champion Lady Base Ball pitcher of the World, will appear in full Base Ball Costume and demonstrate her skill to the entire satisfaction of the audience.

This will probably be the last opportunity for the public to see this female pitching phenomenon and this rare occasion should therefore not be missed.

Hartford Daily Spring, Hartford, MI, May 20, 1908

CHEROKEES AGAIN START SEASON
BY TAKING HARTFORD'S SCALP

The Cherokees, the aggregation of Indian base ball players who emerge from their wigwams at Watervliet every spring to tour the country in a palatial private car and take the scalps of a majority of the baseball teams with which they come in contact, opened the season in Hartford last Friday and as usual took Hartford's scalp as one of the first of the season's trophies. Two games were played, one in the afternoon and one in the evening. The afternoon game was credited to the Indians by a score of 6 to 3, while their victory in the night game was to the tune of 7 to 5. The night game was something of a novelty, the field being brilliantly illuminated and the game being conducted with all the vigor of a day contest. . . .

Watervliet Record, Watervliet, MI, May 22, 1908
CHEROKEES WON GAME
Olson's Indians Were Victorious
in Initial Game at Hartford

This article reports that the Cherokees won their initial game of the 1908 season, 6-2, against Hartford.

Mr. Olson has added a special attraction to his great Indian Club in the person of Maude Nelson, Champion Lady Base Ball Pitcher of the world. The lady pitcher has enjoyed the distinction of being the greatest all-around female ball player in existence. She inaugurated the season of 1908 for the Cherokee Indian Club at Hartford, Michigan, on May 15, by pitching the first two innings of the game and made the remarkable record of retiring the side twice with eleven pitched balls.

It is evident that Mr. Olson intends to produce the greatest Indian Club in the world. HIs ideas are a credit to the base ball profession.

The night game was played under a glare of arc lights to a large crowd. The Indians won out in the ninth inning by a score of 5 to 6.

Mr. Olson leaves here this morning with his ball team for their summer's tour. They will go East and are booked through Canada. They have games booked at Sturgis, Adrian and various other good towns in Michigan en-route to Canada.

Watervliet Record, Watervliet, MI, September 18, 1908
Maud arrived home from the baseball tour and John is expected next week.

1909

Watervliet Record, Watervliet, MI, *January 22,* 1909

This article reports that John Olson put up the Rose Villa Hotel for Sale, Rent or Exchange for City or Farm Property. "Price $3,500. Easy Terms. Or rent $300 per season."

Watervliet Record, Watervliet, MI, March 12, 1909

John receives word that his "right-hand man, Col. Cote," will be there in time to start the season.

Watervliet Record, Watervliet, MI, April 16, 1909

CHEROKEE INDIAN BASE BALL TEAM
J. B. Olson, Jr., Preparing For
Annual Tour, Has New Car

J. B. Olson, Jr. returned from Chicago Tuesday night, where he purchased a fine $3500 Pullman Coach, for the use of his Cherokee Indian Ball Team in its annual tour of the country.

The new car is the finest one Mr. Olson has ever used and he is highly pleased over his bargain.

. . . . Miss Maude Nelson, the famous lady pitcher will travel with the team again this year and pitch two or three innings in each day game.

Mr. Olson is the original traveling ball team man . . . he is planning to play many of the leading semi professional teams in the country.

Watervliet Record, Watervliet, MI, April 16, 1909

Rachel Olson returns from Chicago "and will spend the summer at her son's farm."

Watervliet Record, Watervliet, MI, April 30, 1909

CHEROKEE INDIANS PLAY CHICAGO
GUNTHERS MAY 23

This article reports that John Olson is busy getting his team in order. The Cherokee Indian team was planning to leave Watervliet May 20, with their first game scheduled against the Gunthers at Chicago on May 23. The tour will include

> Mr. Nate Daniels of Kalamazoo, the tallest man in the world. . . . He will go on tour with the team and advertise on the streets the day of the games. T.M. Tracey of Chicago, who will be the contract agent ahead, is also here ready for work. A chef engaged from a Kalamazoo Hotel will be in charge of the culinary department of the car. Ernest Anderson will be chief of the work force and Paul Kreitner will be in charge of the lighting plant.

> Francis Quigno has signed as a member of the team again this season and the other Indian ball players will begin to arrive about May 5. . . .

Watervliet Record, Watervliet, MI, May 14, 1909

This piece reports that the Cherokee Indian team would leave Watervliet that morning, play in New Buffalo the next day and Michigan City the day after. A week from Sunday they would play in Chicago, after which they would start for the East.

Michigan City Evening News, Michigan City, IN, May 17, 1909

OVERTIME BALL GAME SUNDAY
Grays Defeat Cherokee Indians
Score of 5 to 4
INDIANS ARE A FAST AGGREGATION
Maud Nelson of the Indian Nine Performed Duties of Pitcher
During Opening Sessions — Hard Made Hit
That Scored Winning Run

It required ten innings to decide the winner of Sunday afternoon's game between the Cherokee Indians of Watervliet, Mich., and the Michigan City Grays at the latter's park. . . . The Grays scalped the warriors to the extent of 5 to 4. The crowd was the largest seen on the local grounds for several seasons. The fact that the Indians were represented in the pitching department for two innings by Maud Nelson, one of the cleverest woman flingers in the country, proved one of the drawing cards. The locals took advantage of Maud's delivery and countered four times before she was retired in favor of a crack Indian tosser. The Grays were almost helpless before the "pegging" of LeRoy, the Indian brave. . . .

The Cherokee Indians experienced no difficulty in winning from the New Buffalo nine Saturday afternoon in New Buffalo. . . . . The final score was 16 to 5. New Buffalo made 14 errors behind Ritter.

Watervliet Record, Watervliet, MI, June 4, 1909

CHEROKEE INDIANS
OUTCLASS COLUMBIA CITY

This report was from Columbia City, IN, on the May 31 game, Decoration Day. The Cherokee Indian game against the Columbia City Grays drew an immense crowd.

. . . The Cherokees, all of whom except the third baseman are full-blooded Indians, put up an excellent game. . . . The features of the game were the fine fielding of the Indians and Ted Andersen's home run in the fourth inning.

Maud Nelson, an Indian girl, pitched the first three innings, and was so clever with the ball that no hits were made by the Grays in the first three innings.

The article reports that the Cherokees arrived that morning in their railroad car, played a day game, then played a night game using 50 arc lights, each with 1,000 candle power.

Regarding the above article, for those who don't already know, Maud Nelson was Italian, not Native American. In calling Maud "an Indian girl," the reporter was, I hope, referring to her team affiliation.

Regarding the article that follows, I have always wondered whether Cherokee Blanch was really . . . Maud Nelson.

Watervliet Record, Watervliet, MI, October 1, 1909

CHEROKEE INDIANS
HAVE BUM SEASON
John B. Olson Closes Season at Buffalo,
Will Return Home Soon

J.B. Olson, Manager of the Cherokee Indian Base Ball Club, which for several years past he has organized at Watervliet and toured the country with during the summer months, closed the season and disbanded the team at Buffalo, N.Y. a few days ago. Mr. Olson has cleaned up some good bunches of money in the base ball business, but he writes that the past season has been a poor one for travelling ball teams.

Mr. and Mrs. Olson will return to Watervliet soon for a short stay, after which he will go to Chicago to take charge of a new business that promises to be a big winner. The following clipping from the "Bill Board" is explanatory:

Chicago has again produced something new for the benefit of the moving picture houses. This time F.H. McMillan, who has been connected with the film business since the start, is the gentleman who is to be congratulated. Mr. McMillan and Mr. Olson, his partner, have completed arrangements whereby they are able to produce an Indian show for three and four night stands for the different exhibitors on a percentage basis. Cherokee Blanch, formerly with Buffalo Bill, and later with her own show, is the leading attraction. She is the leading shot of her sex and tribe. Besides Cherokee Blanch there are two other acts and approximately 2,000 feet of Indian subjects. The show lasts an hour.

Messrs. McMillan's and Olson's No. 1 Show is meeting with great success. They carry their own advertising matter and give a parade on horseback. This, combined with their ballyhoo never fails to attract the crowds. They intend to put out three shows.

Watervliet Record, Watervliet, MI, October 15, 1909

John Olson returns from Buffalo, NY, and goes to Chicago. "He has sold his car and will dispose of his outfit and go out of the traveling baseball business. Mrs. Olson is visiting friends in Buffalo."

Watervliet Record, Watervliet, MI, December 3, 1909

John Olson was called to Chicago because his father had to undergo an operation for necrosis of the bone at the Reece Hospital. "It will require the removal of his leg below the knee."

1910

Indianapolis Freeman, April 17, 1910

THE ST. LOUIS BLACK BRONCHO BASEBALL CLUB
The Only Colored Female Baseball Club in the World To-Day

This headline appears before a large photo which shows ten people lined up from left-to right. The first four players on the left are men, wearing light-colored baseball uniforms with **STL** visible on the left chest.

Following the four men are six women wearing long-sleeved white shirts without the STL, and dark-colored very full bloomers that stop just below the knees.

UNKNOWN DATES

The following articles are unidentified. I don't know the year, but I'm guessing somewhere between 1908-1915. I could be way off base.

Kentucky Post, May 14

This article reported that the Wiedemann's Brewery team would play a doubleheader at Wiedemann Park. The first game would be against the Covington Standards, then against "the best girl baseball club in the West. . . . To make the attraction more interesting, Miss Nettie Coon, champion lady pitcher of the United States, will be brought here at an enormous expense to twirl against the girl team. . . . She has speed and curves and is as good as any amateur pitcher in this vicinity. The girl team includes Misses Kellar, Mooreland, Meyers, Miller, Becker and Moore."

Perhaps the *Kentucky Post,* May 17

This article reported that "the much-talked-about Miss Nettie Coon" would "display her skill as a pitcher for the Wiedemann team." Further: "Miss Coon twirls in short skirts, while the girls will be dressed in regular baseball suits, nobby and new." In the lineup, Coon did pitch for the men's team.

Perhaps *Kentucky Post,* May 19

This item reports that the Wiedemann team defeated Covington 5-4 but lost to the Bloomer Girls, 6-2.

> Miss Coon, a Dayton girl was on the mound for the Kentuckians and twirled a fine game. The feature of this game was the work of Heitman, one-armed center fielder for the girls' team. He got a triple and double in four times at bat, and made four grand catches of fly balls.

1911

Watervliet Record, Watervliet, MI, February 2, 1911

OLSONS WILL HAVE TWO BALL TEAMS

Mr. and Mrs. J. B. Olson will have two ball teams on the road this season — the Cherokee Indians and the Western Bloomer Girls. Mr. Olson and his Indian team, with Mr. McMillan as advance agent, will start about a month earlier than the Bloomer Girls, from some point in the South. Mrs. Olson has formed a partnership with Miss Kate Becker of Chicago to handle the Bloomer Girls. Both ladies will play in the team, which will start from Benton Harbor or Gary, Indiana, with Mr. Near of Springfield, Ohio, an old-time advance agent, to do the advance work for them. . . . Ernest Anderson and Eddie Olson will go with the Bloomer Girls. Miss Becker was over here Sunday.

After Women at Play *was published I heard from the great-niece of Kate Becker, who said that her mother (Becker's niece) identified Kate Becker in the Western Bloomer Girls postcard, part of which is reproduced as the cover of* Research Notes. *Kate Becker is seated second from right.*

Watervliet Record, Watervliet, MI, April 28, 1911

This article reports that the Western Bloomer Girls Ball Team is managed by Mrs. J. B. Olson of Watervliet and Miss Kate Becker of Chicago, and will open the season at Benton Harbor on April 30.

Watervliet Record, Watervliet, MI, April 28, 1911

This reports that an article from Mrs. Al Coughlin of Chicago, formerly of Watervliet, "sends the following interesting report of the first two games played by the Western Bloomer Girls of Watervliet":

On April 22 the Western Bloomer Girls played the Hammond, Indiana team, score 3-1 Hammond, large attendance. On Sunday they played Indiana Harbor, with over 1500 paid admission.

Wrote Mrs. Coughlin: "All around in the boxes and the grand stand the people were saying they were the best girls' team they had seen and hoped they would come again. Every player is first-class and they certainly put up a good game."

Watervliet Record, Watervliet, MI, May 5, 1911

The Benton Harbor Speed Boys defeated the Western Bloomer Girls the previous week, 8-1. "The girls did some good work, but they have had little practice so far and were outclassed. The game was witnessed by 1,680 people. A large number from Watervliet and Coloma attended the game, Watervliet being the home of Mrs. Olson, one of the managers and the principal player in the team."

Cincinnati Enquirer, July 29, 1911

TYPOS AND BLOOMER GIRLS

The original Bloomer Girls, the team that has been traveling all over the country for the past several seasons and the club that this year has been the talk of the Eastern part of the United States, will arrive in Cincinnati to-morrow morning for a game of ball in the afternoon with the Union Printers, the contest taking place at the Paul Held Park, Earl and Spring Grove avenues, Camp Washington. The young ladies with this team are said to be the most remarkable players for females, and the fact that they have won a large percentage of their games in the East is conclusive proof that they are far from being easy to conquer, and they undoubtedly will make the fast Spinney Leaguers show all they have to get away with a victory. There are seats enough at the Paul Held Park to comfortably seat about 2,000, and judging by the advance demand every available place to witness the game will be taken.

Cincinnati Enquirer, August 21, 1911

While the Bloomer Girls of Boston were playing the Smader Colts in Racine, Wisconsin,, a row of bleachers collapsed, carrying down 300 people.

Watervliet Record, Watervliet, MI, *Watervliet Record,* August 25, 1911

Mrs. J. B. Olson's Western Bloomer Girls, who have been enjoying a most successful base ball tour of the country the past season, are back in Michigan and will play the Detroit Independents at Ramona Park, at Grand Rapids, Sunday afternoon. There is an excursion to Grand Rapids Sunday, $1.00 for the round trip, which will give Watervliet people who desire a good chance to go and see the game.

Watervliet Record, Watervliet, MI, September 1, 1911

WESTERN BLOOMER GIRLS
Enjoy Successful Season. Had Big
Day at Grand Rapids Sunday

The Western Bloomer Girls have played ball with a Grand Rapids team in that city last Sunday. Over 2,000 people turned out to witness the game and the crowd was enthusiastic over clever plays put up by Mesdames Olson & Becker's nine. The score was 2 to 2 at the end of the 7th inning, but the city team scored three more on the girls during the last two innings.

The Bloomer Girls have had a most successful season, and, in fact, are the only traveling base ball team that has made any money this year, says Mr. Olson, who is doing advance work for the girls. He says general conditions in the country have been such that traveling aggregations have had a sorry time of it financially, including his own team, the Cherokee Indians. He says that Michigan and New York are the only two states he has been in where times are good. The following clipping sent us by him is illustrative of conditions:

"This has been the worst season financially, that tented amusement organizations have had to contend with, and showmen from all parts of the country are reporting a decrease of business compared with that of last season. Some of the big ones are changing their routes, while others are planning an early closing. The depression, which now exists, is laid to the unusual hot weather and the long drouth, which has burnt up crops, also discouraged the farmers, which cuts heavily into the revenue of the local merchants. The season has been a disasterous [*sic*] one to many carnivals and circuses, and with no encouraging outlook for the present season, the wise and conservative showmen will probably be in winter quarters not later than the early part of October."

Hartford Daily Spring, Hartford, MI, September 20, 1911

BLOOMER GIRLS COMING
Manager Duffey Signs Girls
for Game Saturday

The Western Bloomer Girls, the girls base ball team that has won from a number of good teams about the state the past few weeks, will meet the Hartford team in a game on the local grounds next Saturday afternoon.

The girls were in town this morning en-route to Paw Paw, and their winsome ways immediately captivated Manager Duffey, who sought an introduction and signed the fair players for a game here Saturday afternoon.

The girls recently played a sixteen inning game with Saginaw, losing by a score of 3 to 2, and have played other equally good games about the state. Should they defeat Hartford it is already assured that the local boys, including L. Jessup and Brayton, will declare that they were too gallant to win.

Gross, the Hartford twirler, has already given bonds as an assurance that he will not blush or become embarrassed. Manager Duffey considered the bonds absolutely necessary.

That the girls will play a good game is certain — but the fans are not so sure of the locals, who are all young men and susceptible to winning smiles.

Among the local fans George Merriman, Ed Hickey, Vol Olds and the editor of this paper have already engaged front seats for Saturday's game. It is a game that every admirer of base ball and amusement, as well as the fair members of the gentler sex, will want to see. The ladies are especially invited to attend the game. The admission price will be 25 cents.

Watervliet Record, Watervliet, MI, September 22, 1911

WESTERN BLOOMER GIRLS
Will Play Coloma at Woodward's Sunday

The Western Bloomer Girls will close the season with a game at Woodward's Ball Park, Paw Paw Lake, Sunday, September 24, with the Coloma team. Maud Nelson will pitch the first four innings, followed by Miss Ruth Woods. They will also play the Hartford team at Hartford Saturday afternoon.

The above article includes a photo of Maud Nelson in a pitcher's pose, dressed in a dark baseball uniform.

Hartford Daily Spring, Hartford, MI, September 27, 1911

BLOOMER GIRLS LOST
GAME WITH LOCALS
Novelty Game Drew Large Crowd
in Hartford — Girls Played Well

In a game that was decidedly the novelty of the base ball season, Hartford defeated the Western Bloomer girls [*sic*] by a score of 6 to 4 last Saturday.

As a clever exhibition of the national pastime the game was not remarkable, but it served to dispel the popular belief that girls can not play base ball.

The locals were intentionally "easy" during the first part of the game, scoring one run in the second inning and holding the score at 1 to 0 until the sixth, when the girls came near "putting one over" on Manager Duffey's champions.

Gross, who had been pitching straight and easy ball, grew too gallant in the extension of his courtesies and the girls rapped out four safe ones which filled the bases with one "girl out."

Clever base running, which disrupted the local organization for the minute, netted the Bloomers four runs. With the score 4 to 1 the local squad never played ball harder than during the balance of the sixth period. Hard hitting soon tied the score, and then they added two more credits for good measure. It was noted, however, that no more opportunities were afforded the girls to put on a wholesale base running speciality.

Maud Nelson, pitcher for the suffragettes, is a really clever twirler and succeeded in striking out a few of the local batters. Mabel Bowers plays her position at first with remarkable cleverness, while Kate Becker at second and Kate Hefferman, Bessie O'Brien and Ruth Woods in the field played a strong game.

At bat the Bloomers displayed signal ability. They wielded the club with all the agility and fearlessness of professionals, and scored more hits than a number of the masculine teams that have opposed Hartford this year.

It was the first game in which the locals have engaged at the Hartford park where they found themselves without the support of the fans. The girls were plainly the favorites and received the applause for their clever plays. It was the one game of the season in which the boys would have been lightly excused had they met defeat. The game was witnessed by a crowd of over 400 people.

Watervliet Record, Watervliet, MI, September 29, 1911
This article reports the Western Bloomer Girl loss to Hartford, 6-4, then reports the game against Woodward.

They played the Woodward team at Paw Paw Lake Sunday. The score-keepers got mixed up and there was a disagreement over the result. The Bloomer fans claim the game 8 to 7 and the Woodwards say they won the game by one. Mr. Olson, manager for the Bloomer Girls, says he believes a correct score would have shown a tie game, 8 to 8.

1912

Watervliet Record, Watervliet, MI, April 26, 1912

The above ad did include the use of "new" twice: adding sic *to the ad would have thrown off the spacing.*

Watervliet Record, Watervliet, MI, May 3, 1912

BLOOMER GIRLS DEFEATED
Lose First Game of Season to
Watervliet By Score of 4 to 1.

. . . . The girls are good players. They have three men in their lineup, the catcher, pitcher and shortstop. Maud Nelson, the champion lady pitcher, only pitched two innings and then Steller took her place.

Thompson was never in danger until the 8th inning, when two bases on balls and two hits gave the Girls one run.

	1	2	3	4	5	6	7	8	9		R	H	E
Bloomer Girls	0	0	0	0	0	0	0	1	0		1	7	3
Watervliet	0	2	2	0	0	0	0				4	13	2

THE BATTING ORDER

BLOOMER GIRLS	AB	R	H	PO	A	E	WATERVLIET	AB	R	H	PO	A	E
Mabel, 1b	4	0	2	5	0	0	Leslie	0	0	0	0	0	0
Bessie, 3b	1	0	0	2	1	0	Jessup	4	0	1	1	0	0
Becker, 2b	2	0	1	2	0	1	Kohlke	4	1	1	2	1	0
Ryan, ss	3	0	1	2	0	Miller	4	1	2	0	2	0
Mary, cf	3	0	0	3	0	0	Hawks	3	0	1	1	0	0
Steller, 2b, p	4	0	2	0	4	1	Lewis	3	1	3	1	1	0
Kittie, lf	3	0	0	1	1	Barden	4	0	1	11	0	1
Florence, rf	4	0	0	1	0	Burke	4	1	2	0	2	0
Gage, c	4	0	0	11	3	0	Smith	4	0	2	10	0	0
Maud, p, 3b	4	1	1	0	1	0	Thompson	4	0	0	1	5	1
TOTALS =	32	1	7	24	13	3		34	4	13	27	11	2

B on B off Thompson 2; off Maud 1; off Steller 1. L on bases Bloom G'ls 8; Watervliet 8. Struck out by Thompson 8, Steller 9. D plays Bloomer Girls 1; Watervliet 1. Hit by pitcher Steller 1; Thompson 1.

Watervliet Record, Watervliet, MI, May 3, 1912
CARD OF THANKS
In behalf of the Western Bloomer Girls I wish to thank the people of Watervliet and vicinity for their liberal patronage of the game last Saturday and for the cordial reception accorded them. J.B. OLSON, JR.

Watervliet Record, Watervliet, MI, May 3, 1912

J.B. Olson, Jr., advance agent for the Western Bloomer Girls, writes from Ligonier, Indiana, that the Girls won the game there by a score of 5 to 3. Ruth got a home run and also pitched the game.

Blount County Journal, Oneonta, AL, May 17 and May 25, 1912

The issues of May 17 and May 24 report that the Al. P. Gibbs ladies baseball team will play in Oneonta and that Miss May St. Leon is the star pitcher. The team travels in a special $10,000 car and has its own canvas fence, 12 feet high and 1200 feet long. The company consists of 20 people. "The organization is composed entirely of highly cultured young ladies and gentlemen — six young ladies and three gentlemen."

Watervliet Record, Watervliet, MI, May 24, 1912

The game between the Watervliet Greys and the Hartford team drew the largest crowd of season with the exception of the Bloomer Girls game.

Watervliet Record, Watervliet, MI, June 14, 1912

John B. Olson, Jr., Advance Manager of the Western Bloomer Girls, was home last Friday.

Mr. Olson says the Girls were up against some bad base ball weather for the first three weeks, but that they are doing fine now. They played to a crowd of 7200 paid admissions at Detroit. They are winning 60 percent of the games. At Vassar they played a 12-inning game, finally winning 5 to 4. They expect to spend about two months in Michigan. Sunday, June 16, they will play at Muskegon.

Watervliet Record, Watervliet, MI, August 16, 1912

"Eddie Olson, who has been traveling with the Western Bloomer Girls, was home this week."

Watervliet Record, Watervliet, MI, October 11, 1912

This article reports that the Western Bloomer Girls played the Loudiens in Chicago on October 6 to a crowd of 2200. It also reports: "Mr. and Mrs. J. B. Olson, Jr., have sold their interests in the team to Miss Kate Becker."

Watervliet Record, Watervliet, MI, October 12, 1912

Mr. and Mrs. J. B. Olson, Jr., and their cousins, John Christopher and Mr. and Mrs. H. Handlen of Chicago, motored over from Chicago in Mr. Olson's car Monday. They left there at 9 o'clock in the morning and arrived in Watervliet at 5:30, using 6-1/2 gallons of gasoline in going 100 miles.

Watervliet Record, Watervliet, MI, December 27, 1912

"J.B. Olson, Jr., has the job of doing the steam fitting for the coating mill. He was in Chicago the first of the week purchasing some material."

1913

Watervliet Record, Watervliet, MI, April 25, 1913

"Mrs. J. B. Olson is getting Rose Villa Hotel at Paw Paw Lake in condition for the summer's business."

Pennsylvania Newspaper, Possible Williamsport or Greensburg, September 13, 1913

LOST TO BRANDONS
A Large Crowd Saw Game At
Athletic Park Yesterday Afternoon
VISITORS PLAYED GOOD BALL FOR FIVE INNINGS
Kate Becker, Woman Pitcher,
Had Drop That Fooled Local Players

Advocates of a Tri-State team for Williamsport were filled with brimming hopes yesterday when they looked over the crowd, both outside and in the Athletic park grounds, gathered there to see the Bloomer Girls, a western nine made up of the eternal feminine, play ball with the Brandon Athletics, a crack local aggregation. One glance showed that the baseball spirit was not dead in Williamsport and that it was alive in a good many breasts.

The Brandons won, 10-4, but the crowd got a run for its money. The Bloomer Girls, presenting Miss Kate Becker, the greatest female pitcher in the world, proved conclusively that women can learn the ins and outs of the national game and that they can line up and battle for nine weary innings when the chances of victory wane every time the cork-centered ball sweeps over the canvas, wafted by an alien bat.

Miss Becker, who was a sort of Man in the Iron Mask or Veiled Princess mystery to some of the crowd, it being confidently asserted on the one hand that she really was a daughter of Eve and on the other that she was masquarading [*sic*] in skirts, or bloomers, pitched Walter Johnson ball. A goodly portion of the onlookers failed to grasp the fact that the nimble Amazon was sending over a drop which broke as sinuously as the strike of a serpent, in the wrapt [*sic*] contemplation of her cap, which was somewhat awry, seeing that the batter stood three balls and two strikes, and of her barrette, which was of last year's design. This same coterie, and it composed a goodly portion of the crowd, failed to realize that baseball is "the business of life" with these women, and that to enter upon that business with the hope of eking a livelihood out of it, they must meet the issue face to face. They must pin their caps close to their heads, and when the only way Garcia gets the message is by sliding to base, they must "hit the dirt."

Of course women playing ball, necessarily, on the ball field, give up some of the things which women in their pursuits have. But they are doing something new, something different: to animate themselves such a sacrifice is necessary. Their conduct on and off the field yesterday was exemplary as ball players. Here the interest of a crowd usually ends when it gets its money's worth. Women just as masculine, although from a different walk in life, are seen on the professional golf links. The Bloomer girls simply get their bread and butter playing ball, to get it they have to leave their powder puffs at home.

Their reliance on the sterner sex was shown by the fact that two or three men appeared in the lineup. Another thing which characterizes the efforts on the ball field of the Bloomer girls is that they don't quit. Although hopelessly beaten they played just as hard in the ninth inning as they did at the start of the game. It is expected that the Newberry team will meet the Bloomer girls some time later in the season.

Katie Walsh, an infielder from Chicago, when asked yesterday how she drifted into the national game, said that she had always liked baseball, and that when a little thing she had played catch with her brother on the lawn. A spirit within her stirred during these impromptu catching matches, which told her that she ought to be a ball player. She sought out Miss Becker, guardian angel of girls who want to play on the diamond — and there you are.

The game yesterday was well enough contested, for five innings the score standing 3-2 in favor of the girls at the beginning of the sixth.

The first baseman for the visitors, who possessed a physique something like Hans Wagner, scooped them out of the dirt, in deluxe manner and if the men on the team had not fallen down would have registered several double plays. As a rule the girls were pretty handy with their gloves, but not quite as effective with their bats. When they got on base they were willing to take chances and they could go some to base. The pitching became a little wobbly after the fifth inning and the jig was up.

The microfilm photocopy of the above article, which I received after Women at Play *was published, is very difficult to read: I have had to guess at several of the smudged words.*

According to people who knew Maud personally, Honus Wagner was a friend of hers. He came to practice with Maud's teams when they were in his part of Pennsylvania. In 1913 the Western Bloomer Girls were owned by Kate Becker: I don't know if Maud played on the team at all in 1913. But I have always wondered if the person possessing the "physique something like Hans Wagner" really was *Wagner.*

1914

Watervliet Record, April 5, 1914

This piece reports that Edward Olson was home from Agricultural College at Lansing for spring vacation.

Watervliet Record, Watervliet, MI, April 24, 1914

There are two separate news items in the same column. The first item reports that John leased his farm to Lon and Will Brooks for the season and that his parents would occupy the house.

The second item reports:

> Mrs. J. B. Olson, Jr., went to Chicago yesterday, where she and Mrs. Figg will organize a girls' base ball team, "The All Americans." Mr. Olson will join her there next week and the team will then leave for a tour of the Northwest with Vancouver, B.C., as the objective point. Mr. and Mrs. Olson have been very successful in their tours of the country with girl ball teams and their many Watervliet friends hope this season will be no exception.

Rose Figg later managed the American Athletic Girls and hired young Margaret Gisolo to play for her. Later Margaret played for Maud Nelson's All-Star Ranger Girls. Notes on Margaret Gisolo will be covered in Volume III of Research Notes.

Watervliet Record, Watervliet, MI, May 1, 1914

The Rose Villa was recently destroyed by fire, and the contract for its rebuilding was let by J.B. Olson Jr. "It is to be a 12-room cottage, two stories with an eight-foot Veranda on three sides."

1916

Watervliet Record, Watervliet, MI, April 28, 1916
"Mrs. J. B. Olson, Jr. has gone to Ohio on a business trip."

1917

Watervliet Record, Watervliet, MI, April 6, 1917
 Maud, "who recently underwent an operation for appendicitis at the Benton Harbor Hospital, was able to return home Wednesday."

Watervliet Record, Watervliet, MI, April 13, 1917
Mrs. John B. Olson, Sr., arrived home from St. Petersburg, Florida, where she had been spending the winter.

Watervliet Record, Watervliet, MI, May 25, 1917

J. B. OLSON, JR.,
TAKEN BY PNEUMONIA

John B. Olson, Jr. died last Monday evening [May 21, 1917], following a brief illness of pneumonia. Mr. and Mrs. Olson went to Chicago a couple of weeks ago and while enroute home on the boat last Wednesday night he was stricken with a sudden and severe attack of that malady. He managed to get home unassisted, but fatal symptoms were immediately apparent. He was delirious most of the time and suffered intensely until the end came.

Mrs. Olson and his son, Eddie, did not learn of his serious condition in time to get here from Chicago before he passed away. Mr. Olson and family have made Watervliet their home for the past fifteen years, although frequently away for several months at a time on baseball enterprises.

He owned a farm on Paw Paw avenue where the Paw Paw Lake Golf Club grounds are located, and a couple of years ago he purchased the Watervliet Garage. He recently leased this property.

Mr. Olson was 44 years old and besides the wife and son is survived by his father and mother, Mr. and Mrs. J. B. Olson, Sr., also of this village. Funeral services were held at the Congregational church Thursday afternoon at 2 o'clock, conducted under the auspices of the Masonic fraternity of which he was a member.

Watervliet Record, Watervliet, MI, June 1, 1917

"Mrs. J. B. Olson, Jr., and her son, Edward, have returned to Chicago."

Watervliet Record, Watervliet, MI, June 15, 1917

Edward M. Olson's name is reported on a list of men who registered for the draft June 5, 1917.

Watervliet Record, Watervliet, MI, July 13, 1917

"Mrs. J. B. Olson, Jr., and Eddie Olson were over from Chicago the first of this week."

After her husband died, Maud returned to Chicago, where she worked in the well-known resort, the Edgewater Beach Hotel, on the north shore of Lake Michigan (within Chicago city limits).

After John's death Maud played with the Boston Bloomer Girls again, and in the early 1920s she managed a women's team for the Chicago Athletic Club, barnstorming New Orleans and the South.

1921

Memphis Commercial Appeal, June 9, 1921

Boston Bloomer Girls Will Play
Local Legion "9"

Memphis baseball fans will be given a novel treat Saturday afternoon at Russwood, when the original Boston Bloomers, the greatest team of female baseball players in the world, will meet the strong local American Legion club. The game will start at 4 o'clock.

The Boston Bloomers have not been to Memphis in some time, but they are well remembered as being one of the best teams of their kind on the road. They are touring the entire country, playing the best teams available. They will reach Memphis early Saturday morning and will parade through the streets of the city prior to going out to Russwood.

The local American Legion team is managed by Walter Long, who promises to put a strong aggregation on the field against the Bloomers. The female ball tossers know how to play ball and it will require a real team to give them a game.

Maude Nelson, who started with the team 20 years ago as the best female pitcher in the game, is now with the team in the capacity of coach and captain.

The lineup of the Legion team will be: Boggan, shortstop; Long, second base and manager; Ferguson, center field; Harris, left field; Atcheson, third base; Brown, first base; Sullivan, right field; Smith, catcher. Ray, Trebing and Wade, pitchers.

The admission will be 50 cents, with the American Legion getting a big share of the proceeds.

Memphis Commercial Appeal, June 10, 1921

In Wilson, Arkansas, the Boston Bloomer Girls "surprised the local fans and the local team also when they defeated the locals this afternoon, score 7 to 0."

Memphis Commercial Appeal, June 11, 1921
Boston Bloomers Will Have
Real Ball Team Here

When the original Boston Bloomer Girls baseball team takes the field agains the American Legion Pastimers Saturday afternoon at Russwood Park, the spectators will see in action an aggregation of female ball players who have perfected the great national game to a remarkable extent, playing the game with the same ability as their brothers. They have been meeting strong clubs all over the country and advance notices are to the effect that they have made a good showing wherever they have appeared.

Maude Nelson, who is the greatest female pitcher in the game, is with the team in the capacity of coach, and has several pitchers whom she is drilling in an effort to enable them to pitch the same variety of ball that she did. Old-time fans remember 25 years ago when the Boston Bloomers first started out that Maude Nelson was quite a hurler.

The American Legion team will be obliged to play all the baseball they can in an effort to beat the female troups, for the girls play real ball, hit like veterans and run bases like professionals. The Bloomer Girls will reach Memphis early Saturday morning and will parade through the principal streets of Memphis just before the game is scheduled to start.

Memphis Commercial Appeal, June 11, 1921

Bloomer Girls Will Play
Legion Team At Russwood Today

The Lineups

Bloomer Girls:	American Legion
Anderson, cf	Boggan, ss
Doughty, lf	Long, 2b
Miller, rf	Ferguson, cf
Sklbens, 1b	Harris, lf
Plaunt, 2b	Atcheson, 3b
Nelson, p	Brown, 1b
Wood, ss	Sullivan, rf
Shepherd, c	Smith, c
Welch, 3b	Ray, Trebing
Sullivan and	and Wade, p
Miller, p	

Whether earnest and continuous practice has made the gentler sex as adept at the game of baseball as their male opponents will be determined this afternoon when the Boston Bloomer Girls, one of the greatest girl teams in the country, will play the local American Legion teams at Russwood Park. The game will start at 4 o'clock and Billy Haack will umpire.

The Bloomer Girls, with their bright red uniforms, reach Memphis this morning, and their manager, Tom Needham, stated that he was expecting his female ball tossers to take the measure of the local boys. "They have been playing fine ball all season and have beaten some of the strongest semipro teams in the country," said Needham, "and they have already stated that they want to add Memphis to their list."

The local American Legion team is one of the strongest arrays of pastimers in Memphis, and is expecting to give the Boston damsels a fast game from the start to the finish. The team is under the management of Walter Long, who also plays second base, and has strengthened several of his positions for today's game, realizing that the Boston girls will be hard to beat.

In the line-up of the Bloomer Girls may be found the names of some of the foremost female pastimers in the game. Maude Nelson, who in her day was a great pitcher, will pitch the first few innings, and then Goldie Miller and Rose Sullivan will adorn the mound. All of them are able to pitch.

For the American Legion club, Ray will pitch half of the game unless he is batted out of the box. Trebing and Wade are available, and if the firing becomes too warm they will get in the game as the Yanks are not counting on letting the girls of the Hub beat them.

The admission will be 35 and 50 cents, with the American Legion sharing liberally in the proceeds.

1922

Times-Picayune, February 23, 1922
Girls Baseball Team to Try to Beat Pros
Miss Birdie Carleton's professional girl baseball team will appear at Heinemann Park Sunday, when they will play Larry Gilbert's Professionals in the first game of a double-header. The game will be a side attraction to the fourth game of the winter baseball series being played between the Professionals and the All Stars.. . .

The first game should be real interesting, as the female team is considered a strong aggregation and will play hard to down the Pros. The bloomer girls have been touring the South playing games in Kentucky, Tennessee and Texas. . . .

Assumption Pioneer [Louisiana], February 25, 1922
"First baseball game of the season Saturday, March 4, at Foley Park; Chicago Bloomer Girls vs. Napoleonville."

Assumption Pioneer [Louisiana], March 4, 1922
Bloomer Girls vs. Napoleonville
"The Chicago All-Star Bloomer Girl Baseball team is scheduled to meet the Naps." No followup score was given.

Times-Picayune, March 15, 1922
PELICANS TO PLAY "BLOOMER GIRLS"

Manager Dobbs found Monday and Tuesday that the task of keeping about thirty young men at work was a little too much trouble without a game, and he determined to arrange a game for Wednesday afternoon.

The Chicago All-Stars, a team made up of women players, is in town and issued a challenge, Dobbs accepting. So the Pelicans this afternoon will meet the "Bloomer Girls," and tomorrow will play the New York Yankees. The "Bloomer Girls" comprise some of the best women ball players in the country and have been seen in action several times in Louisiana towns.

Montgomery Journal, AL, May 7 , 1922

This item announces that the Western Bloomer Girls will play Haleyville on May 9.

Probably *Birmingham News,* May 28, 1922
Goodwater Winner In Game With Girl Team

Goodwater, Alabama, May 27 — The Western Bloomer Girls Team arrived in Goodwater yesterday and played a game with the local team. The game was novel and interesting from the start, and it required 10 innings to determine the winner when the local team won, 7 to 6.

At no time during the game until the final inning did the local team get ahead. Miss Micky McGann was the pitcher for the visitors until the seventh inning, when she was accidentally hit on the head by their second baseman with the ball, which caused her to retire from the game. Up to this time the locals had not made a run and the score stood 3 to 0. Harrison then came to the box and the local team soon located him and batted him freely, tieing the score in the ninth inning. The visitors made another score and the locals, in their half, made two scores, winning the game. If Miss McGann could have pitched all the game, there is no question that there would have been a different ending of the game.

The pitching of Miss McGann, the work of Miss Behle at first base, the homerun of "Rat" Crew for the locals, and the pitching of Aubrey Miller for the local team were the outstanding features of the game.

Montgomery Journal, AL, June 3 , 1922
The Western Bloomer Girls lost to Prattville, 8-2.

Montgomery Journal, AL, June 4 , 1922
The Western Bloomer Girls manager is Miss Kate Becker, a pitcher. "In 1919 she won 105 and lost 51. In 1920 she won 112 and lost 26."

Probably *Montgomery Journal,* AL, June 4 , 1922
The Bloomers tied the Montgomery City League All-Star team 5-5 at Cramton Bowl. The Bloomers had 8 hits, 2 errors,; City Leaguers had 6 hits, 1 error.

More information on Maud Nelson will be contained in Volume III of Research Notes.

Eastern Bloomers: Mostly New York

The New York Bloomer Girls were the best-known such team on the East Coast, formed in Staten Island in 1910 by three local baseball players: Dan Whalen, Joe Manning, and Eddie Manning. In 1914 Margaret Nabel graduated from high school and joined the New York Bloomer Girls: by 1920 she was their manager.

Another well-known Eastern nine was the African-American team, the Black Sox of Baltimore. According to Margaret Nabel, the New York Bloomer Girls played the Black Sox.

The Philadelphia Bobbies, managed by Mary O'Gara, also played the New York Bloomer Girls. Edith Houghton started with the Bobbies at the age of ten, as their shortstop, and toured with the team when it went to Japan in 1925.

From reading the various lineups of teams such as the Quaker City Girls and Philadelphia Bobbies, I surmise that players moved freely between the two teams. Edith Houghton played not only with the Bobbies, but also with the New York Bloomer Girls, most likely using a different name. Mary Gilroy [later Mary Gilroy Hockenbury] also played for more than one of these various teams.

1915

New York Age, June 3, 1915

This item in the sports pages report that the New York Bloomer Girls beat the Clinton freshmen, 6-4.

		R. H. E.
N.Y. Bl'm'r Girls	0 1 0 0 0 1 0 3 1 —	6 10 4
Clinton Freshmen	0 0 1 0 1 2 0 0 0 —	4 11 3

Batteries — Miss Demerest and Joe Wall; Walsh and Williams.

1920

Philadelphia Inquirer, June 11, 1920

"Marshall E. Smith defeated the Bloomer Girls of New York yesterday in a twilight game by 7-3."

Philadelphia Inquirer, July 6, 1920

New York Bloomer Girls

Beaten by Bridesburg A.A.

"Bridesburg A.A. defeated the Bloomer Girls 16-2 [*sic*] before 8000 people. "

Bridesburg A.A.	r	h	o	a	e
Mann, 2b	3	2	0	2	0
Shouldt, 1b	1	1	0	0	0
Cleary, lf	3	3	14	0	0
Butts, c	0	1	1	2	0
Keenan, rf	0	3	0	0	0
Moser, cf	0	1	1	0	0
Diamond, 3b	3	4	2	3	0
Comfort, ss	1	4	0	2	0
Hoffman, p	1	2	0	0	0
Totals	16	24	27	7	0

N.Y. B. Girls	r	h	o	a	e
P'kers, 2b	0	1	0	1	1
Andres, 3b	1	1	1	2	0
Friss, 1b	0	1	10	0	1
Gilroy, lf	0	0	1	0	0
Thorpe, ss	0	0	2	3	0
D'risk, rf	0	0	1	0	0
Roth, cf	0	1	2	0	0
Magee, c	2	2	6	0	0
Ustalfi, p	0	1	1	1	0
Totals	3	7	24	7	2

Bridesburg A.A.	2 0 3 0 0 4 4 3 x —	16
N.Y. Bloomer Girls	0 0 1 0 0 2 0 0 0 —	3

The Gilroy who played left for New York was probably Mary Gilroy, who played for a factory team in Philadelphia, the Fleisher Bloomer Girls.

Probably S*taten Island Advance,* April 27 or 28, 1921

New York
Bloomer Girls

Champion Female Baseball Players of the World with Toots Andres, the Babe Ruth of the team; Stella Friss and other stars to play

Tappen Post

Sunday, May 1st at 3 o'clock at East Shore Oval Stapleton

S*taten Island Advance,* April 30, 1921

TAPPEN POST NINE TO PLAY
N.Y. BLOOMER GIRLS TOMORROW

East Shore Oval promises to be the scene of considerable excitement and interest tomorrow afternoon when the Tappen Post baseball team hooks up with the New York Bloomer Girls, acknowledged champion female athletes of the East.

Says the Girls' manager, Margaret Nabel of Stapleton, "We have already stowed away two fine games this season, having played at Wilmington, Del., two weeks ago and at Vernon Oval in

Bay Ridge two weeks ago Sunday. Although we lost both games by a 6 to 3 score, our girls put up splendid games in both places and we were highly complimenting [*sic*] on the showing made.

"Our last appearance on Staten Island was in 1919, when we played the Downey Inter-departmental team at Sisco Park, and it will be remembered that we led the Downey's a merry chase before they finally beat us out in an interesting game by a 12 to 9 tally. Since that time, we have played a great many games. Last season, for instance, we covered a total of 3500 miles in our 32 games played, in various parts of the States of New York, Pennsylvania, Connecticut, Maryland, Vermont, and at Montreal, Canada. In 25 of these games we established records for attendance and receipts, and did not fail to give satisfaction in any of the games played.

"We have met many strong semi-pro teams, such as the Baltimore Dry Docks team, the same collection of stars which trounced both the Assumption Caseys and the Downey Shipyard nines last Fall at Sisco Park. We played the Dry Docks twice last year, one game at Coatesville, Pa., and we made such a splendid showing that we were taken to the International League Grounds at Baltimore and drew the biggest crowd of paid patrons that had ever been to any game between semi-pro teams in Baltimore. The game was full of thrills and 'pep' and the Dry Docks handed up a 9 to 8 trimming, much to our regret. However, we understand that they usually won about 9 out of every 10 games they played, so it really was not such a bad showing, was it?

"The team is practically the same as that which played at Sisco Park against the Downeys, excepting in a few positions: Stella Friss is on first base. Rose Kane at second, Toots Andres at short and Rose Roth at the far corner. Helen Demarest, a Stapleton girl, by the way, will be in left. Roselyn Pelsner in center, and Betty Gaber in right field. We use a male battery exclusively, as we feel that no female player can do justice to the pitcher's burden, and you will agree that the catching job belongs to a man, too.

"Our star is Stella Friss, captain and infielder extraordinary. Stella will show Staten Island fans how far women have really advanced in the realm of sport for she can knock the apple a mile and plays the initial bag a la Hal Chase when that once superlative player was in his prime. Toots Andres at short, is probably a more finished infielder than Stella, and her delight is to grab a hot liner without the quiver of an eyelash, even using her ungloved hand if the occasion demands. Her ability to scoop 'em up and get her man at first will delight the fans, and we predict that on more than one occasion Toots will get her share of the applaus [*sic*] for fine plays made.

"We are booked six weeks ahead, having games at Metuchen, Bayonne and Ridgewood in New Jersey; Wayne, Easton, Catasauqua, York and Philadelphia Pa; College Point, L.I.; two games at Baltimore, Md., and are working on an extensive tour through Pennsylvania, especially in the vicinity of Pittsburgh and probably in a few of the towns in Ohio bordering on Pennsylvania. "We are out to win our games, just the same as any other team, but if we happen to lose on Sunday we feel sure that the Tappen Post team will know it has been in a real game before we finish with them."

East Shore Oval is being put into first class playing shape for tomorrow's game and an attempt will be made to have seating arrangements ready. The Post is endeavoring to put baseball on a firm footing in Stapleton, and all members are hard at work bosting [*sic*] their favorite team.

Staten Island Advance, June 18, 1921

Added strength to the Tappen Post outfit tomorrow will be seen in Eddie Manning, one of the best second basemen ever developed on Staten Island. Eddie has been taken on in the capacity of coach and while it is not certain that he will play himself, his presence on the bench as head coach will add much to the Tappen Post forces. Few wiser heads every played on Staten Island than the old Alaska and Sisco star.

Philadelphia Inquirer, August 5, 1921

BLOOMER GIRLS BEATEN
Jack Himes' Old Timers Defeat Lassies
by 9 to 5 Score

Jack Himes Old-Timers defeated the Quaker City Bloomer Girls, 9 to 5. A large crowd turned out to see the game, including quite a few of the fair sex., who rooted hard for the girls.

Miss Gilroy covered first base as good as her big brother and short stop Miss Jaegers covered herself with glory with her many good stops and throws.

Playing for the Old-Timers were: Murphy, Willsman, Peltz, Shafer, Borns, Short, Wakeley, Walsh, Simons, and Hol. Playing for the "City Girls" were: Russell, Jaegers, Stafford, Weaton, Conway, Knies'r, Wilson, Gilroy, Daly, Miller, and McBride.

Baltimore Afro-American, August 12, 1921

GIRL NINES PLAY BALL
The Black Sox Bloomers Lose To
Excelsior Girls of Sparrows Point
17 to 14
ENDS IN PROTEST
Hostilities To Be Resumed
Thursday at Black Sox Park

What turned out to be a real baseball game was staged at Druid HHI Park last Thursday afternoon when the Black Sox Bloomer Girls defeated the Excelsior Girls of Sparrows Point 17-14. In addition to the large number of Sparrows Point and Bloomer Girls rooters, a large number of spectators were on hand. The smile on the faces of many of the disinterested onlookers showed that they were of the impression that the game would be a joke, but before it ended they had been agreeably surprised.

It was the first contest of the season for the Black Sox Bloomer Girls, while their opponents have been playing for about a month.

In the 9th inning the Bloomer Girls brought the spectators to their feet. The first batter up hit a hot grounder to short which Miss Johnson grabbed and threw the batter out several feet from the bag. The next batter met one of Miss Taylor's outshoots on the nose and it started for centerfield. It only started — Miss Taylor took it right off the bat. She was given a rousing cheer. The third batter was thrown out at first by Miss Johnson in the same snappy manner that she had tossed out the first batter.

In their half of the 9th the Bloomer Girls went on a batting rampage and slamming the pellet all over the lot in such fashion that although they had come up in this inning trailing the visitors 12 to 17, before the latter were aware of what had taken place, two runners had crossed the home plate and two were on base waiting for just a half-chance to do likewise. It was at this point that the visiting team protested a decision of umpire Greyer's and the game ended with both sides arguing the point. The teams will meet in another game at Westport Ball Park next Thursday (Aug. 18th) and settle the question of superiority.

I received articles on the Black Sox after Women at Play *was published. A box score follows the above article, but my microfilm photocopy is too smudged to read.*

Baltimore Afro-American, August 19, 1921

S.P. Bloomer Girls
Win Another Game

Sparrows Point, MD. AUG. 17 —On last Saturday the Excelsior Bloomer Girls of Sparrows Point smothered the Oak Dale Bloomer Girls of North Point, Md., 25 to 5, before a large crowd of enthusiastic spectators.

The Score.

Oak Dale G.	Ab	r	h		Excelsior G.	Ab	r	h
Redd, ss	6	0	2		Waters	7	4	4
Snord'n, 2b	6	1	3		Winston	7	4	2
Buril, cf	6	0	0		U. Wilson	7	2	4
Locky, 3b	5	0	0		P. Wilson	6	2	2
Burwell, rf	5	0	0		Brooks	6	2	2
Redd, c	5	0	0		L. Jones	6	3	4
Wallace, lf	5	2	1		Brown	6	1	2
Parker, 1b	5	1	2		O. Wilson	6	4	2
Gregory, p	5	2	1		F. Foster	6	2	1
Totals	48	5	9		Totals	58	25	25

SCORE BY INNING

Excelsior Girls.	4 3 3 3 1 3 2 4 2 —	25
Oak Dale Girls	0 0 0 0 1 0 2 1 0 —	5

Two base hits — Everybody on Excelsior, Snordum, Redd, Licky. Sacrifice — F. Winston, 2: O. Wilson, 3. Home Runs — L. Jones, 2; Foster, 1: C. Harris, 1. Base on balls — Winton, Brooks, Foster, U. Wilson. Stolen bases — Winston, Wilson, Wilson, Wilson, Waters. Strikeout — G. Jones, 17: S. Gregory, 4. Umpire — Harris and Johnson.

Baltimore Afro-American, September 9, 1921

GIRLS NINES FIGHT
ANOTHER CLOSE BATTLE
Black Sox Bloomer Girls Defeat
Excelsior Girls of Sparrows Point

The Black Sox Bloomer Girls journeyed to Sparrows Point last Thursday and defeated the Excelsior Girls of that place 32-31 in another sizzling contest: the third which these teams have engaged in this season.

It was plain from the outset that the visitors were suffering from stage fright, this being their first trip away from home. How much so may be gathered from the fact that at the end of the 5th inning the Black Sox Girls were trailing the Excelsior Girls 8-25. But when this fright had worn off the B.S. Girls got busy, and when the game ended they had forged out on the long end by one tally.

The features of the game were the batting of Miss Clarke and a triple play by the Misses Forster, Marshall and Johnson.

Two new players have been added to the Black Sox Girls' team, namely: Miss M. Crockerall who will play 1st base and Miss F. Williams who will chase flies in the left garden.

On the 15th of this month these teams will head up once more at Maryland Park, Westport.

The microfilm photocopies of the articles from the Baltimore Afro-American *were difficult to read. They contain box scores, but I couldn't decipher some of them. If you are researching the names of the players or the statistics of the game, you should request the microfilm itself.*

1922

Staten Island Advance, May 11, 1922

Downey Baseball Team Will Play
Host to Bloomer Girls This Sunday

This article reports that a double header would be played, the 3:00 game featuring the New York Bloomer Girls vs. the Downeys, with the Bronx Lodge of Elks vs. the Staten Island Elks scheduled for 4:00.

The article goes on to say that on the previous Sunday the New York Bloomer Girls opened up a new ball park at South Norwalk and drew a capacity crowd. In the last three seasons, they have played north as far as Montreal and south as far as Richmond, VA.

"Miss Friss is the female Babe Ruth and she certainly can clout the ball. Last Sunday in South Norwalk Stella got three hits, a single, a two-bagger and a triple. She often hits for the circuit. The Girls have a male battery and have a good pitcher in Bob Mullin."

Staten Island Advance, May 15, 1922

Tom Shehan's Downeys added the New York Bloomer Girls to their list of victims by defeating them in the first game at Sisco park yesterday afternoon by the score of 8 to 1.

The Girls' team has a male battery and short stop. Mullen fanned 7 Downeymen while Allie Van Pelt turned back eight of his opponents after three swings at the air. The Downeys started scoring and got six runs in the fourth. Van Pelt got a life on an error. Lunny walked. Roe doubled, scoring Van Pelt and Lunny. Mullusky singled and Clark doubled, scoring Roe and Mullusky. Thompson singled, scoring Clark. Ruggles fanned. Olsen singled, scoring Thompson; Grosjean walked but Van Pelt, up for the second time this inning hit into a double play.

In the fifth the Sheehanites added two runs on four free passes, a passed ball and two base robberies.

The Bloomer Girls scored their only tally in the fifth when Corcoran got a life on an error, Nabel singled and Van Pelt hit Engrant, filling the bases. Mullen fanned; Paton walked, forcing in one run. Demarest fanned, ending the inning.

Nabel and Corcoran were the only ones who got hits on the Girls team.

The score by inning:

Bloomer Girls.	0	0	0	0	1	0	0	—	1
Downeys	0	0	0	6	2	0	x	—	8

Unknown Source, August 9, 1922

BLOOMER GIRLS BAT OUT 6 TO 4 VICTORY

Broomall Damsels Spank Boy Friends,
Winning Out in Last Inning

Media, Pa. July 8 — Broomall Bloomer Girls, succeeded in beating the Broomall Club, at Broomall today by the score of 6 to 4. The game was a part of the Fourth of July programme, which was postponed on account of rain.

The game was preceded by field sports for the young folks, but the ball game between the young men and girls was the main attraction.

The game was featured by the pitching of Miss Hannah Watson, and the batting by Mrs. Howard Everett and Pauline Culbertson.

A box score accompanies the above article, but it's too smudged to read.

Although I don't know the source or dates of the items below, my guess is that the first three games occurred in 1922. Edith Houghton, whom the items report as being 10 years old, was born in 1912, so she would have been ten in 1922.

Unknown Source

The Philadelphia Bobbies played a 9-inning game against the Morton Bloomer Girls. The pitcher, Miss Russell, fanned 17 batters in six innings. Edith Houghton was 10 years old.

Unknown Source

INDIANS WIN FARCE

Locals Take Comedy Game from Female Team at Rossmere, 17-15

This article reports that a game between the Philadelphia Bobbies and the Lancaster Indians went only 7 innings. Despite being required to bat left-handed, the Indians collected 20 hits, many of them extra-baggers. The Bobbies collected 13 hits. "Little Miss Houghton, the 10-year-old phenom, covered plenty of ground at shortstop for the visitors and made herself a favorite with the fans by her splendid fielding and ability at the bat."

Unknown Source, Jenkinton

The article reports that the Bobbies lost a close one to Jenkintown, 9-8, with a big crowd attending. Agnes Forrest hit a homer, a double, and two singles in four trips to the plate. Houghton, 10 years old, had seven chances, one error.

Unknown Source, Baltimore, July 27

BOBBIES BEATEN

This item reports that 6,000 fans saw the Tinicum Bloomer Girls defeat the Bobbies, 24-11.

1923

The Literary Digest, July 28, 1923

Under the Sports and Athletics report is a piece stating that women are gaining on men in basketball, "offsetting man's natural superior wight by their greater natural agility and team-work." It states that the Kansas City Bloomer Girls played a New Jersey semipro men's team and won the game.

Staten Island Advance, September 12, 1923

BLOOMER GIRLS IN BIG SERIES:
HELEN DEMAREST PITCHES NEW YORK GIRLS
TO VICTORY OVER PHILLY GIRLS.

"The New York Bloomer Girls won the first game of a series to decide the female championship of the East last Sunday at Howard Field in Brooklyn, defeating the Philadelphia Girls Athletic Club by a 21 to 13 score, before an enthusiastic crowd of 2000 fans."

The article reports that Helen Demarest, whose team scored 11 runs in the first inning, remained steady on the mound, never extending herself. Florrie O'Rourke and Toots Andres did well for the Bloomer Girls, as did Mary Gilroy and Ada Jaggers "for the Quakertown lassies."

The second game of the series will be in Philadelphia on September 15, the third game at the Bronx Oval on September 30.

Unknown Source

This article reports that the Philadelphia Bobbies team starts its season April 18. The team had been working out for a month, helped by several big league players before they departed for camp. The leading pitcher is Edith Ruth. Floss Eakin, catcher, is one of best hitters, a fast runner and track star. Almost the entire team played basketball. First base is Jennie Phillips, second base Alma Nolan, an expert swimmer. The Bobbies shortstop is Edith Houghton, who is 11. Third base is Stella Law; right field, Edna Rush, known as "Home Run Baker." Center field will be Mary O'Gara, manager, and one of the team's best players.

I'm assuming that the above article is from 1923 because Edith Houghton is reported to be eleven years old.

1924

Staten Island Advance, April 29, 1924

This item reports that Margaret Nabel's sister, Miss Emma Nabel, of 50 Beach Street, Stapleton, had accepted a position with Metropolitan Life Insurance Co. in Ottawa, and that her parents hosted a party for her.

Unknown Source, Unknown Date,

A postcard depicts the New York Bloomer Girl team seated.

The top row consists of: Toots Andres, Florrie O'Rourke, Stella Friss, Helen Demarest, Betty Gaber.

In the middle row: Youngstrum, Margaret Nabel, manager Poole.

In the bottom row: Mary Slater, Edna Kouri.

Youngstrum and Poole were the men on the team. They wore light-colored uniforms and striped sox. The women wore black uniforms with white trim and striped sox.

Poole played short, Youngstrum was the catcher. Kouri, 2b; Andres, 3b; Friss, 1b; Gaber, cf; O'Rourke, rf; Slater, lf; Demarest, p; Nina McCuttun, utility; Mary McGown, utility; Mary Knapcsek, utility.

1925

Staten Island Advance, August 15, 1925

This is an obituary for Carl Nabel of 50 Beach street — Margaret Nabel's father. The funeral services were conducted by Rev. Jacob Ganss, pastor of St. Paul's Deutsche Evangelische church in Perth Amboy. Internment was in the Moravian Cemetery in New Derp. Carl Nabel was 66 years old.

Staten Island Advance, September 9, 1925
BLOOMER GIRLS TO PLAY METS SUNDAY
Margaret Nabel's Female Stars
Should Attract Season's Greatest Crowd

This three-paragraph article informs readers that the New York Bloomer Girls would play Harold Doyle's Metropolitan Giants, who, until Labor Day, had not been defeated.

"The Girls have not played on the Island in some time and they should be in for a hearty welcome. All of the old time favorites are till in the lineup." The item opines that the Bloomer Girls' strong male battery "will help silence the Mets bats."

Staten Island Advance, September 12, 1925

METRO GIANTS WILL OPPOSE BLOOMER GIRLS AND TIGERS MARGARET NABEL'S FAMOUS COLLECTION OF FEMALE BALL TOSSERS WITH MALE BATTERY WILL PLAY FIRST GAME. JACKIE HAYES WILL PITCH FOR TIGERS

This is a lengthy article which repeats some of the New York Bloomer Girl history from previous long articles. It praises Nabel as a manager, calling her "the female Jaws McGraw."

"Some of the girls have been playing as long as ten years, which will give an insight into the seriousness with which they take the game."

The article states that the New York Bloomer Girls average more than 50 bookings a season throughout the East, and that many teams rebook them for the following year. According to the report, the Bloomer Girls played from Montreal to Virginia, and "as far west as Ohio" against semipro male teams.

Staten Island Advance, September 12, 1925

A photo of the team appears under the caption, "Bloomer Girls Play Here Tomorrow."

The photo shows nine female players plus Margaret Nabel. The players are arranged according to height, shortest to tallest, left to right, with Nabel as the last figure.

Each player is wearing a dark-colored uniform with the word "York" visible on the left side. Each player has a number on her sleeve. Margaret Nabel is wearing a light-colored skirt and jacket and cloche hat.

Left to right the players: Ethel Condon; Edna Kouri; Toots Andres; Helen Demarest, Captain; Mae Knapesek; Nina McCuttun; Elsie Duhnke; Florrie O'Rourke; Gean Whalen; Margaret Nabel, Manager since 1919.

Unknown Source

BOBBIES ALL SET FOR ORIENTAL TOUR

This article reports that by 1925 the Philadelphia Bobbies team had been "a unit" for three years, and that their name came from their bobbed hair. "The Bobbies are bobbies."

The Bobbies would be traveling to Seattle, from which point they would depart for Japan on a baseball tour. Further, the piece reports that eight games have been arranged for the trip across the U.S., "bringing the team to Seattle on October 6, where they will sail the same date for Yokohama, Japan. The Bobbies will boost the Sesqui-Centennial on their way, and they will wear uniforms of blue and yellow, the city's colors."

According to this article, former major league catcher Eddie Ainsmith and his wife were the team's official chaperons.

More articles and information on Edith Houghton and the Philadelphia Bobbies will appear in Volume II of this series. More information on the Bobbies trip to Japan will appear in Volume III.

1927

Unknown Source, May 18, 1927

BARNSTORMING CATCHERETTE

A photo two columns wide shows a woman in full baseball gear, with shin guards, chest protector, and catcher's mitt, hat on backwards. The caption reads: "The Philadelphia Bobbies — an all-girl baseball team — is to tour the United States, meeting twenty feminine teams. Mickey Robinson (above), is the Bobbies' mainstay behind the plate."

Unknown Source, May 19, 1927

FEMININE ROGERS HORNSBY

This item is probably from a New York state newspaper, possibly even New York City. Two pictures of Maggie Riley are contained in a boxed feature. One shows Riley hitting, the other shows her leaping straight up for a ball. In the second photo, the words MAGGIE RILEY are visible on the front of her uniform. The item states that Riley is the "first base lady" for the New York Bloomer Girls.

1929

Staten Island Advance, October 25, 1929

This is an obituary of Mrs. Margaret Nabel, mother of the Bloomer Girls manager. Mrs. Nabel was survived by seven children and had been a resident of Staten Island for more than twenty years.

1930

Staten Island Advance, September 17, 1930

BLOOMER GIRLS BACK AFTER LONG BASEBALL TOUR
Margaret Nabel Is Again
Claiming Title for Popular Team

This long article states that the Bloomer Girls were on the road for sixteen weeks, having covered 1,150 miles, as follows: New Jersey, Maryland, Delaware, Virginia, New York, Pennsylvania, Vermont, Massachusetts, New Hampshire, Maine, New Brunswick, Nova Scotia, and Prince Edward Island.

This year's Bloomer Girl tour was booked by Nat C. Strong.

Three female ball teams are reported to have challenged the New York Bloomer Girls for "female baseball championship of the East," though the article mentions only the "Philadelphia Bobbie Girls" by name.

The article also states that the "ever-reliable battery of Helen Demarest, pitcher, and Toots Andres, catcher, will again be called on."

Infielders were listed as Maggie Riley, Mae Rohr, Ethel Condon, and Babe McCuttun. Outfielders were listed as Ruth Doyle, Evelyn Lynch, Peggy O'Neil, and Margaret Nabel "ready for outfield duty."

I infer from the above that the New York Bloomer Girls may have retained a male battery when playing against men's teams, but used a female battery when playing other women's teams.

Staten Island Advance, October 2, 1930

MARGARET NEBEL'S [*sic*] BLOOMER GIRLS
TO PLAY AT TRENTON
Meet Philadelphia Bobbies in What
May Be Final of Series

This long article reports that the second of a three-game series in the "female world series" would be played against the Bobbies in Trenton, NJ, on Sunday, October 5. The New York Bloomer Girls won the first game 16-6. "It leaked out later that the star pitcher of the Bobbies, Miss Elsie Rockhill of Bristol, Pa., had pitched nine full innings the day previous and was naturally not in prime condition."

"Miss Demarest pitched only four innings against the Bobbies the first game, after which Ruth Doyle and Margaret Nabel each pitched two of the remaining innings." Babe McCuttan hit a double and a triple and drove in six of the sixteen runs.

The star player for the Bobbies was Agnes Robinson.

Margaret Nabel was confident that a third game would not be necessary. The article concludes: "this is the 20th consecutive baseball year for the New York Bloomer Girls, during which time they have never been defeated by another female club, a record of which the players are very proud of. [*sic*]"

The two articles that follow, from the Trenton Times, *were, I believe, misdated by whoever sent them to me. (The handwriting isn't mine.) The two articles are marked* "1930," *but when read with the article above, they make no sense in terms of date and number of games and victories in the mentioned series.*

Possibly the Staten Island Advance *article was misdated, but I think not.*

My guess is that the two articles below actually have a 1931 or possibly 1932 date.

Trenton Sunday Times, October 5, 1930

PHILA. BOBBIES TODAY OPPOSE BLOOMER GIRLS.
Feminine Tossers Meet at Dunn Field for Mythical Title

This long article reports: "The mythical women's baseball championship of the world will be at stake this afternoon when the Philadelphia Bobbies oppose the New York Bloomer Girls at 3 o'clock on Dunn Field."

The Philadelphia Bobbies had just won the Quaker City series against a Passaic team. The article lauds the Bobbies' battery: "Titian-haired Agnes Robinson, catcher extraordinary, lives so close to New Jersey that she could almost be claimed by the Garden State. Miss Robinson, 19-year-old lass, hails from Morrisville, Pa." The pitcher was Elsie Rockhill, 17 years old, from Emilie, Pennsylvania.

"Miss Rockhill has a drop and a fast pitch. The combination of Rockhill and Robinson was the downfall of the Chicago Bloomer Girls, who trouped the East all summer opposing men's teams in exhibition matches. The Windy City outfit condescended to match their skill against the Philadelphia Bobbies recently and were defeated decisively."

Mary O'Gara was the Bobbies manager.

Trenton Evening Times, October 6, 1930

BLOOMER GIRLS DEFEAT BOBBIES
First of Series for Title
Is Taken by New York Team

This article reports that the New York Bloomer Girls won the first game of "the mythical women's baseball championship" series, defeating the Philadelphia Bobbie Girls at Dunn Field, 12-9.

The Bobbies scored seven runs in the second inning to lead the game, "but the hard hitting Bloomer Girls cut away at this big lead until four runs in the fifth put them ahead to stay."

Margaret Nabel was the starting pitcher for the Bloomer Girls, "but was shelled off" the mound, to be replaced by Helen Demarest. Elsie Rockhill pitched for the Bobbies.

The second game might be the following Sunday at Cadwalader Park.

1931

Staten Island Advance, April 4, 1931

WHY GIRLS LEAVE HOME FOR THE BASEBALL FIELD
Veteran Woman Player Who Has Swatted
Ball in 20 States Concedes Men Are Best Sluggers

This very long article on Margaret Nabel and the New York Bloomer girls recounts the history of the team and gives Margaret's opinions on whether women can compete against men as baseball players. Nabel says they cannot.

According to the article, Nabel is known as "Baseball's Woman Pioneer."

The second paragraph informs that the Chattanooga, Tennessee, Southern League club signed female Jackie Mitchell recently.

The New York Bloomer Girls were formed in 1910, organized by Dan Whalen. During the same year, Ida Schnall, "famous aquatic star and athletic luminary," formed the Empire City Girls to compete against the Bloomer Girls. But her team soon faded.

"A girl can develop a slow curve, an effective floater, good control and perhaps everything else that a good male player can show, except speed," Nabel said.

"While I wish my Tennessee colleague every success, it seems it is just another publicity stunt," Nabel opined.

Nabel is very proud of the longevity of her team. Other female baseball teams listed as examples of those that came into being and soon went out of existence include: "Boston Bloomer Girls, Quaker City Girls, Fleischer Yarn Girls of Philadelphia, General Electric Girls of Schenectady, Troy Collar League Girls, Philadelphia A. C. Girls, Wilmington Rubber League Girls, Eastman Kodak Girls of Rochester, Stetson Bloomer Girls of Philadelphia, Heath Silk Girls of Scranton, and Baltimore Black Sox Colored Girls."

The article also quotes Nabel on how difficult it is to find, train, and keep female players. Some players spoil their chances of becoming regular team members by being "big-headed."

A large part of the article concerns Nabel's opinions about the various places the New York Bloomer Girls have played ball, ranging from Nova Scotia to Florida.

1932

Staten Island Advance, April 4, 1932

BLOOMER GIRLS TEAM
SEEKS LOCAL OPPONENT

This two-paragraph article states that Margaret Nabel, manager of the New York Bloomer Girls, would like to book a game for the next Sunday, "with a local Light Senior or Big League team."

The New York Bloomer Girls would start their season on April 17 in Parlin, New Jersey, "meeting the Holy Trinity Club at Du Pont Oval."

Staten Island Advance, April 7, 1932

BLOOMER GIRLS TO PLAY ON SUNDAY

This four-paragraph article reports that the New York Bloomer Girls would open their season on Sunday, against West Babylon A.A., of the South Shore League.

The next week, the Bloomer Girls would participate in another opener, against the Holy Trinity Club at DuPont Oval in Parlin, N.J.

"The New York Bloomer Girls will play practically all their games within a 100-mile radius of New York City this season, giving every team of any consequence an opportunity of presenting this novel attraction to their fans. . . ."

1933

Staten Island Advance, April 1, 1933

BLOOMER GIRLS PREPARE FOR ANOTHER BIG SEASON
Margaret Nabel to Give Island Girls Chance to Make Team

This seven-paragraph article announces that the New York Bloomer Girls will again field a team, and that even though they played all of last season's games within a 100-mile radius of New York City, they managed to play 82 games last season.

According to the report, the Bloomer Girls in the past traveled "as far as Texas and Mexico."

". . . the season was ended in a blaze of glory when Margaret Nabel's players decisively won a championship victory from Edith Houghton's Philadelphia A.C. team at the new Bayonne City Stadium before the largest crowd ever to see a baseball tilt at that park."

The article lists some of the male teams the Bloomer Girls beat last season, including Ted Poole's Fordham Lyceum, Tom Davies' Caldwell, N.J., Komets, and others.

There would be changes in this year's New York Bloomer Girls roster.

" . . . the biggest surprise last season was the phenomenal progress made by Hattie Michaels of Bayonne, who joined the team as a possibility and soon crowded the well-known Maggie Riley off first base." Other Bloomer Girl members: Helen Demarest, Madge Simmons, Dottie Ruh, Babe McCuttun, Billie Taylor ("the sensational left-handed basketball star of Union City Reds Girls fame"), Ginger Robinson, Ruth Harper, and Mel Pearsall.

By 1933 most Bloomer teams had disbanded: people simply couldn't afford to attend games during the difficult years of the Great Depression. It appears that 1933 was the last season for the New York Bloomer Girls.

1934

Standard-Sentinel, Hazleton, PA, May 1, 1934

This item reports that the Paterson Bloomer Girls of New Jersey would play at Tigers' park in Freeland.

Standard-Sentinel, Hazleton, PA, June 1, 1934

PIERCE GIRLS' TEAM TO PLAY
JEDDO AT FREELAND SUNDAY

This article reports that "the famous Pierce Girls' baseball team of the New York Girls' Club" would face the Jeddo Stars at Tigers' Park in Freeland.

The Pierce Girls were all women, no men on the team. "Madge Cassidy, the only girl in existence to ever accomplish a no-hit, no-run pitching performance against a masculine team," would take the mound against Jeddo. Marie Pinetta would catch.

The infield for the Pierce Girls consisted of: Grace Doria, Beatrice Zondella, Madeline Schwing, Marie LaMorte. The outfield consisted of Margaret Schlett, Anna Dudeldich, and Ruth.

"The girls claim the female baseball championship of both New York and New Jersey."

1935

Staten Island Advance, April 1, 1935
SEEKS PLACE ON TEAM
Below the large headline is two-column photo of a young woman wearing a baseball uniform and wielding a bat. The caption states that the coach of a high school in Webster, Massachusetts, has promised Nellie Twardzik a place on the team "if she continues to perform as well as she has in early practice sessions. She's a regular Babe Didrickson at first base."

1985

Boston Globe, November 8, 1985
Agnes Rogers, 80,
Former pro baseball player
This obituary states that during the Great Depression Agnes Rogers "played first base for several teams, including the Hollywood Girls, the Chicago Girls and the New York Girls, and maintained a lifelong interest in sports."

Rogers was called "Aggie O'Neil" when she played. According to a friend, Rogers met Babe Ruth during one of her team's tours, and "he gave her a ring right off his finger."

Roger worked at Fenway Park, Boston Garden, and Sullivan Stadium "as a matron."

My Darling Clementine

The article below was first published in New City: Chicago's News & Arts Weekly, *the May 2-8, 1996 issue.*

Only two things slowed my discovery of who Maud Nelson was.

Her name wasn't Maud.

Her name wasn't Nelson.

My hunt for Maud Nelson, the most renowned Bloomer Girl of the early era, began seven years ago as research for a book on women who played baseball. From two sentences in a book and two in a thesis, I started with these facts: Maud Nelson, famous pitcher, played for the Boston Bloomer Girls in 1898 and the Chicago Stars in 1902.

Taking the information at face value — that Maud Nelson did pitch, that she was famous — I expected that with a little library work I would learn all about her.

Three months and countless card catalogs and magazine indexes later, I had turned up nothing. Turning to the National Baseball Hall of Fame Library in Cooperstown, I requested copies of the materials in their early-women-in-baseball file. Clippings from the *Cincinnati Enquirer* and a few other papers dating from 1898-1911 proved that Maud Nelson (sometimes spelled Maude, sometimes Neilson) did pitch for various Bloomer Girl teams.

Usually comprised of seven women and two men, bloomer teams played against men's nines, barnstorming from coast to coast by train. In the early years, the teams Maud Nelson played for barnstormed from Florida to Maine, Kentucky to Oregon, with long stops in Ohio and Indiana.

Wherever she went, Nelson earned the respect and praise of fans and sportswriters. A 1905 game in Lewiston, Maine, was typical. According to *The Boston Herald:* "The feature of the game was the pitching, batting and fielding of Miss Neilson. She made three base hits, and had four put outs and four assists and made no errors. In the five innings she pitched she struck out seven men."

What I was learning was exciting, but the going was slow. When I asked research advice of Sharon Sliter Johnson, a friend and fellow writer, she volunteered to work as my research assistant. Sharon's father had played in the minor leagues, and she was avidly interested in both research and women in baseball. On the day we agreed to hunt for Maud, neither of us anticipated that the search would burrow into our psyches and stay with us forever.

We checked various biographical volumes. We enlisted the aid of English and Scandinavian historical societies, "Neilson"indicating either nationality. Because so many baseball players of that era were Irish, we also checked Irish-American societies, and because Maud played for the Boston Bloomer Girls and the Chicago Stars, we checked city directories in both Boston and Chicago, then expanded to Cincinnati and Portland. Each search came up empty.

I moved forward, researching other ballplayers — players such as Mary Gilroy Hockenbury, born 1903 in Philadelphia. At the age of fourteen Mary started her ballplaying on the factory-sponsored Fleisher Bloomer Girls.

On a cold January morning, with snow driving against my window in Chicago and piled on lawns in Philadelphia, I interviewed Mary by phone. As she reminisced, she told me that in 1922 she had received a letter from Maud Olson of Chicago, asking her to play on a bloomer team that would train in New Orleans.

Maud.

"Do you mean Maud Nelson?" I asked.

"No," she replied, "I think it was Olson."

I asked whether the Maud Olson she knew had ever been a baseball player. No, she answered. A pitcher? Not to Mary's knowledge.

Logic told me Maud was a common name at the time. A hunch told me there was only one Maud.

Seeking more information on Mary's ballplaying, I requested microfilm of the 1922 *New Orleans Times-Picayune.* When it arrived in March, I read that the Chicago All Star Athletic Girls were in New Orleans, managed by Maud Nelson. Not Olson, but Nelson. This was the woman I wanted.

It appeared that Mary Gilroy Hockenbury had remembered incorrectly, but she still led me to an exciting discovery: a pitcher in 1897, Maud Nelson was a manager as late as 1922. That's 25 years on the green grass of baseball fields. That kind of presence, especially for a woman, indicated not only an intense love of baseball, but steadiness, commitment, and success. Clearly, Maud Nelson was more than a pitcher in 1898 and 1902. Just how much more remained to be discovered.

By May my desk was covered with dozens of newspaper clippings from 1928, when 14-year-old Margaret Gisolo of Blanford, Indiana, helped lead an American Legion Junior team to the state championship. The story of this second baseman who batted .429 in the playoffs and made ten putouts and 28 assists would form an exciting chapter in my book. After interviewing Margaret, professor emeritus of the Department of Dance at Arizona State University, I promised that I would call as more questions occurred to me, and she promised she would answer.

Many months later (the following year, in fact), Margaret wrote to say that, by the way, she had played baseball with Maud Olson's All-Star Ranger Girls out of Chicago from 1930-34. Immediately I telephoned. "Maud Olson?" I asked. "Could it have been Maud Nelson?" Margaret replied no, it was Maud Olson — of that she was certain.

What was going on? I couldn't accept that *both* Margaret Gisolo and Mary Gilroy Hockenbury misremembered the name of their team owner. Disturbed by the discrepancies between my hunch and the *Times-Picayune* on one hand, and the testimony of Mary and Margaret on the other, I called Margaret back. What did she remember about Maud, I asked. She thought a while. Maud was quiet. Competent. Often she traveled ahead to book games. Maud was married, said Margaret, and her husband, John, traveled with the team.

I telephoned Mary Gilroy Hockenbury and asked if the woman she remembered as Maud Olson was married. Mary thought a while, then said that Maud (the 1922 Maud) talked about her husband, John, but Mary had never seen him. Mary's lasting impression was that Maud had been a widow.

The paradoxical recollections of Mary and Margaret (husband John dead in 1922, alive in 1934?) baffled me. Sharon and I retraced previous steps, asking ethnic and historical societies to check for Maud *Olson*, not Nelson. Once again, the result was zero: no such person existed in the files of any society we consulted.

Week after week, month after month, we kept looking. In a 1923 Chicago city directory, Sharon saw three Maud Olsons listed. One of these lived at 936 Leland Avenue, worked as a maid, and was the widow of John. Was this the woman we wanted — the pitcher of 1897, the manager of 1922, and the owner of 1934? Did Maud Nelson have a 37 year span in the national pastime?

And always the unanswered question: who *was* Maud?

Approximately two years after I'd begun my research, I visited Cooperstown. There I found a photocopy of a postcard of Maud Nelson. At last, I could *see* the person I searched for.

Maud is dressed in a dark knickerbocker baseball uniform with a light stripe down the side of the pant leg. She is wearing dark baseball stockings (no stirrups) and baseball shoes. Her left hand sports a baseball glove. Her right hand grips a ball, her right arm pulled back as if to pitch. On her head is a baseball cap, its visor so short that Maud's dark hair, twisted and tucked up into her cap, all but obscures it. She looks short for a pitcher. Her face is squarish, with a wide mouth, straight nose, and dark eyes. Maud Nelson looks serious: full of purpose.

Excited by the discovery, I mailed copies of the postcard to Mary and Margaret, asking each if this was the woman she knew as Maud Olson. Both were positive it was. I was now convinced that Maud Nelson and Maud Olson were one and the same, and that she was the single most important person in the first fifty years of women in baseball.

Rain whispered against my window early one September morning when the phone rang. Margaret Gisolo telephoned to say she had been hunting through boxes in her woodshed and discovered a letter written to her brother Toney in February of 1929. Imprinted with the name "Maud Nelson Olson," the stationery bore the address 4918 Sheridan Road, Chicago. In the letter, Maud gave Toney a bank reference in Watervliet, Michigan, in case he wanted to check on her financial reliability.

I rushed to my car and drove up Sheridan to find the house. Maud Nelson, whom I had looked for in more states than could fill a lineup, once lived thirty-three blocks north of my apartment.

But 4918 was no longer there, replaced by a newer building or different numbering system. Wherever I went, it seemed as if I had just missed Maud.

Sharon, meanwhile, called the Watervliet Public Library and learned from librarian Cindy Young that: (1) there was a women's baseball team in Watervliet early in the century, and, (2) bound volumes of the *Watervliet Record* were stored in the library's back room. Sharon and I made arrangements to drive to Michigan.

Naturally it rained the day we left. Shedding our raincoats, we sat down with bound volumes of the *Record,* Sharon to research 1912 and work forward, I to research 1911 and work backward.

What we learned in one morning was all new to us: John and Maud Olson were prominent citizens of Watervliet; John was known as "the baseball man" and fielded a barnstorming team called the Cherokee Indian Base Ball Club, composed of Native Americans; Maud formed the Western Bloomer Girls ball team, co-owned by herself, John, and a Kate Becker of Chicago, with Maud and Kate functioning as player-managers.

After a quick lunch, we decided that I would continue to hunch over the heavy volumes of the *Watervliet Record* while Sharon would brave the rain to case the town and check records at City Hall.

From the 1909 newspaper I learned that John and Maud had a son, Eddie Olson, who during summers often traveled with the Cherokee Indian Base Ball Club. Sometimes the *Record* referred to him as "Mrs. Olson and her son Eddie," sometimes "his son Eddie," making me wonder whether Eddie was Maud's stepson. I also learned that John B. Olson, Sr., and his wife Rachel lived in the same household as John, Maud and Eddie.

Intriguing bits of the barnstorming life filled the yellowed pages. John Olson owned a Pullman car, *Clementine,* in which his teams traveled. The *Record* reported that the car would "carry eleven Indian base ball players, besides four canvas men and the proprietors and their wives and all will eat and sleep on the car." The Pullman's undercarriage held a 1200'-long and 12'-high canvas fence "for use in towns that have no enclosed grounds."

Sharon returned. Folding her umbrella, she removed her raincoat and shook it out, managing to look ebullient and uneasy at the same time. Her first stop had been an antique shop, where she found two identical postcards of the Western Bloomer Girls and one of Maud Nelson — the very image I had seen in the Baseball Hall of Fame.

The photo of the Western Bloomer Girls was the best bloomer photo we had yet discovered. The team consisted of eight women, two men, and a female booking agent or manager or chaperone (it's difficult to tell which). The players wear traditional baseball uniforms: gray flannels with a cursive **WBG** embroidered on the shirt. Five women are seated cross-legged in the front row; the back row of players is standing. They all look comfortable. Relaxed. They look like they live to play the game.

Sharon's elation over discovering the postcards was well-founded. Unfortunately, so was her unease. She had stopped in City Hall, which sent her to the morgue. There she learned that a John B. Olson had died in 1917 and was buried in the Watervliet Cemetery. "That can't be Maud's husband," she beseeched. "He's too young." Armed with the date of death, we turned to the May 25, 1917 *Watervliet Record* to check obituaries.

There a front-page article confirmed our dread: John B. Olson, Jr. died suddenly from pneumonia contracted while crossing Lake Michigan.

Dusk enveloped the library as Cindy Young led us to the Watervliet cemetery to find John's grave, for there also we would find Maud Nelson.

With October drizzle beading our clothes, we stood on the grass of the six-grave Olson plot, staring at John's tombstone, conscious of the fact that Maud Nelson once stood on this very dirt.

The other five graves were empty. Neither John's father nor mother were buried there, nor his son, nor his wife.

Once again, Maud Nelson demanded that we search for her. Somewhere, she was waiting for us.

Driving home to Chicago, we considered what we had found. It seemed strange that the senior Olsons wouldn't be buried with their son. It seemed strange that Maud wouldn't be buried with her husband. Had she married again, and was she buried with her second husband? Or had she left with Eddie and was she buried with him? The trail led back to Chicago, for that's where Maud was living in 1929, when she wrote to Toney Gisolo.

And Mary Gilroy Hockenbury had remembered correctly — the Maud Olson she knew in 1922 was a widow, and her husband's name had been John.

But Chicago provided no further leads to Maud, so in January we resumed our trips to Michigan, where we at least had the *Watervliet Record*. Because John's obituary had identified the Olsons as residents of Watervliet for fifteen years, I determined to discover when they moved there, and from where. Sharon worked her way forward from 1917, trying to discover when they left.

A 1907 issue yielded the information that Maud, Eddie, and Maud's nephew, Alphonse Brida, returned from Chicago. The discovery of a new family name excited me: the more names, the greater our chances of finding Maud Nelson. Possibly Maud had a sister who married a Brida.

On alternate Wednesdays, each of them rainy, we made the drive to Watervliet. One Wednesday I reached 1905 and learned that John, Maud, and family moved to Watervliet in February, arriving by train from Chicago Heights, Illinois. But checking of the Chicago Heights directories revealed neither Nelson nor Olson nor Brida.

Brida. We couldn't find the name in any phone book. What nationality was it? I couldn't find it in any book on name origins. It certainly didn't sound Irish. Or English, or Scandinavian. To Sharon I posed a question: what if it wasn't Maud's sister who married a Brida, but ... what if Maud's own name were Brida? What if she Americanized it to play baseball — a common phenomena of the times. Sharon countered that perhaps Maud married somebody named Nelson — perhaps she was married before she married John Olson.

Thoughts of Maud coursing through me, I worked daily on the book that would become *Women at Play: The Story of Women in Baseball.* By this time I had reached the 1940s and was interviewing players of the All-American Girls Baseball League.

Whenever possible, Sharon and I would meet at the Chicago Historical Society to check city directories. The 1928-29 phone book indicated that Elmer Brida resided at 4918 N. Sheridan Road — Maud's address. Unfortunately, this led nowhere.

We also found the Olsons during the 1890s, up to 1905. John B. Olson Sr. and his son were steamfitters. They moved around from year to year, living on the city's near west and near north sides. In 1923, Edward M. Olson appeared in the city directory, residing at 936 Leland — the same address as Maud Olson, widow of John. And in 1929 Maud's in-laws, John Sr. and Rachel, lived with her at 4918 Sheridan Road. By that time, Edward M. Olson had disappeared from the phone book, leading us to believe he probably moved away — to the suburbs or beyond.

Eddie Olson seemed an important key to Maud Nelson. If he was her natural son and born around 1900, there was a very slight chance he was still alive. If he was her stepson and born earlier, he still may have had children and grandchildren.

Finding him took time. I was well into the 1950s when Sharon called one morning to say that an obituary she requested had finally arrived.

Edward Martin Olson was born in Chicago on February 20, 1895, his father John Benjamin Olson, Jr., his mother Lena Boe. On May 20, 1923, he married Edna Reimers, who died in 1971. Their son Donald died in 1972. In December of 1976, Eddie Olson died at the age of 81. The paper said he was buried in Graceland Cemetery.

I drove to Graceland, where written records indicated Eddie was buried in the same plot as John Sr. and Rachel. The grave was difficult to locate, its limestone markers weathered, the chiseled names barely discernible. Although the name of

Edward Olson wasn't cut into a headstone, cemetery records listed him as buried there. The trail of Eddie Olson seemed to stop.

But many weeks later, Sharon received another obituary — one which reported that Eddie Olson was survived by a half-brother, Howard Schick.

Calling libraries and funeral homes, Sharon learned that Howard Schick had died only six months earlier, survived by his children. Through them, she received confirmation that Eddie and Howard were half-brothers, that Lena Boe and John B. Olson, Jr., had divorced, and that Eddie had come to visit his mother in Chicago as a boy and young man. But the Schick descendants knew nothing else about John B. Olson, Jr., and nothing about Maud Nelson.

The sky gray, sharp rain tapping at the windows, we returned to Watervliet. As we had so many times before, we walked into the single-story brick building and nodded our greetings to librarians Cindy Young and Wanda McLain. Arranging our notebooks on one of the two long tables near the front desk, we walked back to the storage room and pulled out two volumes of the *Record.*

Minutes later, Sharon let out a whoop. Peering over her shoulder, I read in the January 4, 1929 issue of the *Watervliet Record:* "Mrs. Maud Olson Dellacqua was over from Chicago a couple of days the latter part of last week on business and called on old friends here." A November 1929 issue contained this item: "Mrs. Maude Olson Dalacqua and her brother, J.B. Brida, were here from Chicago over the week end." Then, in an October 1931 issue, Sharon found this: "Mrs. Maud Olson Dallacqua and her stepson, Joseph Dallacqua, motored over from Chicago today and called on local friends."

Maud Nelson Olson had remarried, and we now knew the last name (though not its correct spelling!) of her second husband. We knew Maud's birth name as well — Brida. And the name of a second stepson: Joseph. What would we find when we looked up "Dellacqua" in the Chicago phone book?

We found somebody by that name at an address around the corner from me. He confessed he had never heard of Maud Nelson, but he did know a Joe Dellacqua — his grandfather, who lived in the suburbs. We dialed Joe Dellacqua and asked him if he was the stepson of Maud Nelson. "Oh, Maud!" were his first words. "Sure. Maud owned a baseball team."

There it was. The words "Maud" and "baseball" uttered naturally in the same sentence: permanent association. We had followed the footsteps for years, had stood on the dirt of graves, had searched in places far and near, and now a person who knew Maud Nelson intimately was alive and willing to talk to us.

Joe Dellacqua was perhaps ten years old when Maud married his father, Costante, a widower. He remembers that Maud and Costante met at the Edgewater Beach Hotel, where Costante was a chef and she worked in the cafeteria. Maud raised Joe and he, like Eddie before him, got to travel with a baseball team when one day around 1926 or 1927, Maud said to his father, "Let's start a baseball team."

Thus the All-Star Ranger Girls that Margaret Gisolo played on were born, with Maud and Costante as owners. Maud and Joe drove ahead as booking agents and Costante (whom the players called John — hence Margaret Gisolo's memory of Maud being married to John was also correct!) stayed with the team.

The name "Brida" was Italian, and Maud was born in the Austrian Tyrol. She came to America with her father and brothers. Joe thought she grew up in Chicago, but wasn't sure. He had no idea how Maud acquired the last name of "Nelson."

During one conversation, Joe's wife Evelyn said to me in an off-hand way, "You know her name wasn't Maud."

It figured that the woman I now knew as Maud Brida Nelson Olson Dellacqua would test me once again. "What was her name?"

"Clementine," answered Evelyn.

Maud Nelson died on February 15, 1944, at the home she and Costante had lived in for ten years, not far from Wrigley Field. She is buried in Graceland. From where I live, I can walk there. One rainy day in February, Sharon and I met to locate the burying place of Maud Nelson.

It's a single grave, for Costante returned to Italy after Maud died and is buried there. The gravestone is enduring granite, though nobody has visited the site in decades. She is buried near the Olsons. "Sister & Wife, Clementina B. Dellaqua, 1879-1944" is chiseled into her tombstone. The last name is misspelled, and the birth date may not be correct, for her social security records list it as November 17, 1881 and her death certificate as February 15, 1874. As I placed a bouquet of carnations across the gravestone, I knew there would always be something new to discover about Maud Nelson.

A baseball should be carved into the granite. The game was in her blood. She played it professionally for decades, making pitching appearances as late as 1922, when she was 41 years old. She pitched for men's teams and women's teams, played third base in late innings, scouted players, managed teams, owned them and then sold them, increasing the number of successful bloomer teams. If it hadn't been for Maud Nelson, hundreds of women would never have been able to play baseball — hardball: the real thing.

She had the ability to look deep inside people and see if they had the right stuff. She picked out Margaret Gisolo for the All-Star Ranger Girls. And back in 1934, she picked out Rose Gacioch, an eighteen-year old wanna-be from Wheeling, West Virginia, took her barnstorming, and made a player out of her. Ten years later, Rose Gacioch would sign with the All-American Girls Baseball League and go on to an eleven-year career with the Rockford Peaches.

Maud Nelson's influence extended beyond her lifetime. She was a hero, and I'm honored that I was the one to find her.

I bequeath myself to the dirt to grow from the grass I love,
If you want me again look for me under your boot-soles.

You will hardly know who I am or what I mean,
But I shall be good health to you nevertheless,
And filter and fiber your blood.

Failing to fetch me at first keep encouraged,
Missing me one place search another,
I stop somewhere waiting for you.

— Walt Whitman, "Song of Myself"